Would **You** Kill the Fat Man?

Would **You** Kill the Fat Man?

The Trolley Problem and

What Your Answer Tells Us

about Right and Wrong

David Edmonds

Princeton University Press

Princeton and Oxford

Library of Congress Cataloging-in-Publication Data

Edmonds, David, 1964–
Would you kill the fat man? : the trolley problem and what your answer tells us
about right and wrong / David Edmonds.
pages cm
Includes bibliographical references and index.
ISBN 978-0-691-15402-2 (hardcover : alk. paper)   1. Ethics.   2. Thought
experiments.   3. Churchill, Winston, 1874–1965—Miscellanea.   I. Title.
BJ1012.E34 2013
150–dc23   2013012385

British Library Cataloging-in-Publication Data is available

This book has been composed in Electra and Syntax

Printed on acid-free paper. ∞

Printed in the United States of America

10 9 8 7 6 5 4 3

To Liz, Isaac, and Saul
(an undiscriminating fan of wheels, trains, and trolleys)

"Clang, clang, clang" went the trolley
"Ding, ding, ding" went the bell
"Zing, zing, zing" went my heartstrings
From the moment I saw him I fell.

—*Hugh Martin and Ralph Blane,*
"The Trolley Song," 1944
(sung by Judy Garland in Meet Me in St. Louis*)*

Contents

PART 4 The Trolley and Its Critics

Figures

Prologue

The levity of the examples is not meant to offend.

—Philippa Foot

THIS BOOK IS GOING TO LEAVE in its wake a litter of corpses and a trail of blood. Only one animal will suffer within its pages, but many humans will die. They will be mostly blameless victims caught up in bizarre circumstances. A heavyset man may or may not topple from a footbridge.

Fortunately, almost all these fatalities are fictional. However, the thought experiments are designed to test our moral intuitions, to help us develop moral principles and thus to be of some practical use in a world in which real choices have to be made, and real people get hurt. The point of any thought experiment in ethics is to exclude irrelevant considerations that might cloud our judgment in real cases. But the experiment has to have some structural similarities with real cases to be of use. And so, in the forthcoming pages, you will also read about a few episodes involving genuine matters of life and death. Making cameo appearances, for example, will be Winston Churchill, the twenty-fourth president of the United States, a German kidnapper, and a nineteenth-century sailor accused of cannibalism.

Thought experiments don't exist until they have been thought up. Books covering philosophy tend, rightly, to focus on ideas, not people. But ideas do not emerge from a vacuum; they are the product of time and place, of upbringing and personality. Perhaps they have been conceived as a rebuttal to other ideas, or as a reflection of the concerns of the moment. Perhaps they reflect a thinker's particular preoccupation. In any case, intellectual history is fascinating, and I wanted to weave in the stories of one or two of those responsible for the ideas on which this book is based.

There is a reason why the crime at the heart of this book, the killing of the fat man, has never been fully solved, philosophically: it is complicated . . . really complicated. Questions that, at first glance, appear straightforward—such as "When you pushed the fat man, did you *intend* to kill him?"—turn out to be multi-dimensional. A book that attempted to address every aspect of all the fraught issues raised by the killing would be ten times the length of this one. In any case, although some of the intricacies can't be avoided—indeed, they provide much of the scholarly excitement—my aim was to write a book that did not require readers to hold a philosophy PhD.

When I first came across the trolley problem I was an undergraduate. When the fat man was introduced to philosophy I was a postgraduate. That was a long time ago. Since then, though, what has reignited my interest has been the perspective brought to bear on the problem from several other disciplines.

My hope is that the text that follows will give some insight into why philosophers and non-philosophers alike have found the fat man's imaginary death so fascinating.

Acknowledgments

THIS IS A DULL BIT FOR THE READER, but a welcome opportunity for the author—the acknowledgment of debts. And I have a trolley load of people to thank.

First, to numerous philosophers: I've conducted many interviews or had many meetings with academic philosophers about the book, and have also drawn on relevant material gathered through my work with the BBC, *Prospect*, and especially *Philosophy Bites* (www.philosophybites.com). These philosophers include Anthony Appiah, Fiery Cushman, Jonathan Haidt, Rom Harré, Anthony Kenny, Joshua Knobe, Sabina Lovibond, Mary Midgley, Adrian Moore, Mike Otsuka, Nick Phillipson, Janet Radcliffe Richards, Philip Schofield, Walter Sinnott-Armstrong and Quentin Skinner.

Second, thanks to another set of philosophers who have read part or all of the manuscript. No doubt there are still errors in the book, but that there aren't more of them is down to Steve Clarke, John Campbell, Josh Greene, Guy Kahane, Neil Levy, John Mikhail, Regina Rini, Simon Rippon, Alex Voorhoeve, and David Wiggins (and Nick Shea, for helping me decipher Professor Wiggins's handwriting).

Third, thanks to those who assisted with material for the biographical section—Lesley Brown, M.R.D. Foot (who, sadly, has passed away), Sir Anthony Kenny, and Daphne Stroud, a former tutorial partner of Philippa Foot's.

Fourth, I appreciate assistance I received from journalists at the BBC and *Prospect*. Colleagues at the BBC were crucial during this book's germination stage. Jeremy Skeet helped to commission a two-part BBC World Service series on the subject, which was presented by the estimable Steve Evans, an economist with an insatiable curiosity, who would have made an excellent philosopher. For the past few years I've been contributing philosophy articles to *Prospect*, in which some of this material was given a first airing. James Crabtree (now of the *Financial Times*) and the former editor, David Goodhart, commissioned articles on subjects that other periodicals would shy away from. If it's possible to plagiarize one's own work, then I'm guilty in one or two places of doing so. The chapter on experiments in philosophy relies on some of the research done for an interview, co-written with Nigel Warburton, on the X-Phi movement. And I've also written for *Prospect* on enhancement as well as on the trolley problem itself.

Fifth, to the team at Princeton University Press: Hannah Paul and Al Bertrand were patient and encouraging throughout the writing process—people always express similar sentiments about their editors in the acknowledgment section, but this time it's really true. Copyeditor Karen Verde, illustrator Dimitri Karetnikov, and press officer Caroline Priday made up an excellent team. Hannah Edmonds, as usual, played the role of proofreading long-stop, brilliantly catching grammatical and spelling infelicities that had slipped through others.

Sixth, thanks to my agents at David Higham, particularly Laura West and Veronique Baxter.

Seventh, my referees' input was much appreciated. Princeton approached two academics to read the manuscript. I was fortunate in that both of them are moral philosophers of international standing and both chose to waive their anonymity.

Roger Crisp, a professor at Oxford, made numerous useful suggestions, as did Jeff McMahan, of Rutgers and Princeton and one of the world's leading specialists in this area.

Eighth, gratitude to Julian Savulescu, Miriam Wood, Deborah Sheehan, Rachel Gaminiratne, and others at Oxford's Uehiro Centre for Practical Ethics, for providing me over the past several years with such an hospitable academic base. Likewise, to Barry Smith and Shahrar Ali from the Institute of Philosophy.

Ninth, thanks to Britain's finest Indian restaurant, the Curry Paradise, for fueling the brain.

Finally, several friends merit a special mention. For the past six years, Nigel Warburton has been my partner-in-crime on the *Philosophy Bites* podcast. As of May 2012, our interviews have had 18 million downloads: more important, the series has been tremendous fun and has given me a wonderfully broad philosophical education. I also want to acknowledge two non-philosophers. John Eidinow (with whom I've written three books) and David Franklin, a law scholar, are very clever chaps indeed. Both read the entire manuscript and made countless invaluable comments.

The book is dedicated to Liz, for her loving kindness and her gentle toleration; to Saul, who has trumped my trolley pre-occupations with his toy-train obsession; and to Isaac, the most delightful of way stations, born some time between chapters 7 and 8.

PART 1

Philosophy and the Trolley

Churchill's Dilemma

AT 4:13 A.M. ON JUNE 13, 1944, there was an explosion in a lettuce patch twenty-five miles south-east of London.

Britain had been at war for five years, but this marked the beginning of a new torment for the inhabitants of the capital, one that would last several months and cost thousands of lives. The Germans called their flying bomb *Vergeltungswaffe* — retaliation weapon. The first V1 merely destroyed edible plants, but there were nine other missiles of vengeance that night, and they had more deadly effect.

Londoners prided themselves on — and had to some extent mythologized — their fortitude during the Blitz. Yet, by the summer of '44, reservoirs of optimism and morale were running dry, — even though D-day had occurred on June 6 and the Nazis were already on the retreat on the Eastern front.

The V1s were a terrifying sight. The two tons of steel hurtled through the sky, with a flaming orange-red tail. But it was the sound that most deeply imprinted itself on witnesses. The rockets would buzz like a deranged bee and then go eerily quiet. Silence signaled that they had run out of fuel and were falling. On contact with the ground they would cause a deafening explosion that could flatten several buildings. Londoners tempered their fear by giving the bombs a name of childlike innocence: doodlebugs. (The Germans called them "hell hounds" or "fire dragons.") Only an exceptional few citizens could be as phlegmatic as the poet Edith Sitwell, who was in the middle of a reading when a doodlebug was heard above. She "merely lifted her eyes to the ceiling for a moment and, giving her voice a little more volume to counter the racket in the sky, read on."[1]

Because the missiles were not piloted, they could be dispatched across the Channel day or night, rain or shine. That they were unmanned made them more, not less, menacing. "No enemy was risking his life up there," wrote Evelyn Waugh, "it was as impersonal as a plague, as though the city was infested with enormous, venomous insects."[2]

The doodlebugs were aimed at the heart of the capital, which was both densely populated and contained the institutions of government and power. Some doodlebugs reached the targeted zone. One smashed windows in Buckingham Palace and damaged George VI's tennis court. More seriously, on June 18, 1944, a V1 landed on the Guards Chapel, near the Palace, in the midst of a morning service attended by both civilians and soldiers: 121 people were killed.

The skylight of nearby Number 5, Seaforth Place, would have been shaken by this explosion too. Number 5 was an attic flat overrun by mice and volumes of poetry: there were so many books that additional shelves had had to be installed in what had originally been a bread oven, set into the wall. There was a crack in the roof, through which could be heard the intermittent growl of planes, and there were cracks in the floor as well, through which could be heard the near constant roar of the underground. The flat was home to two young women, who shared shoes (they had three pairs between them) and a lover. Iris was working in the Treasury, and secretly feeding information back to the Communist Party; Philippa was researching how American money could revitalize European economies once the war was over. Both Iris Murdoch and Philippa Bonsanquet would go on to become outstanding philosophers, though Iris would always be better known as a novelist.

Iris's biographer, Peter Conradi, says the women became used to walking to work in the morning to discover various buildings had disappeared during the night. Back at the flat, during intense bombing raids, they would climb into the bathtub under the stairs for comfort and protection.

They weren't aware of it at the time, but matters could have been worse. The Nazis faced two problems. First, despite the near miss to Buckingham Palace, and the terrible toll at the Guards Chapel, most of the V1 bombs actually fell a few miles south of the center. Second, this was a fact of which the Nazis were ignorant.

An ingenious plan presented itself in Whitehall. If the Germans could be deceived into believing that the doodlebugs were hitting their mark—or, better still, missing their mark by falling north—then they would not readjust the trajectory of the bombs, and perhaps even alter it so that they fell still farther south. That could save lives.

The details of this deception were intricately plotted by the secret service and involved several double agents, including two of the most colorful, ZigZag[3] and Garbo.[4] Both ZigZag and Garbo were on the Nazi payroll but working for the Allies. The Nazis requested eyewitness information about where the bombs were exploding—and for a month they swallowed up the regular and misleading information that ZigZag and Garbo provided.

The military immediately recognized the benefits of this ruse and supported the operation. But for the politicians it had been a tougher call. There was an impassioned debate between the minister for Home Security, Herbert Morrison, and Prime Minister Winston Churchill. It would be too crude to characterize it as a class conflict, but Morrison, who was the son of a policeman from south London and who represented a desperately poor constituency in east London, perhaps felt more keenly than did Churchill the burden that the operation would impose on the working-class areas south of the center. And he was uneasy at the thought of "playing God," of politicians determining who was to live and who to die. Churchill, as usual, prevailed.

The success of the operation is contested by historians. The British intelligence agency, MI5, destroyed the false reports dispatched by Garbo and ZigZag, recognizing that, were they ever to come to light, the residents of south London might not take kindly to being used in this way. However, the Nazis never improved their aim. And a scientific adviser with a stiff upper lip, who promoted the operation even though his parents and his old school were in south London ("I knew that neither my parents nor the school would have had it otherwise"), estimated it may have saved as many as 10,000 lives.[5]

By the end of August 1944, the danger from V1s had receded. The British got better at shooting down the doodlebugs from both air and ground. More important, the V1 launching pads in Northern France were overrun by the advancing Allied forces. On September 7, 1944, the British government announced that the war against the flying bomb was over.[6] The V1s had killed around six thousand people. Areas of south London—Croydon, Penge, Beckenham, Dulwich, Streatham, and Lewisham—had been rocked and pounded: 57,000 houses had been damaged in Croydon alone.

Nonetheless, it's possible that without the double-agent subterfuge, many more buildings would have been destroyed—

and many more lives lost. Churchill probably didn't lose too much sleep over the decision. He faced excruciating moral dilemmas on an almost daily basis. But this one is significant for capturing the structure of a famous philosophical puzzle.

That puzzle is the subject of this book.

Spur of the Moment

How are they free from sin who . . .
have taken a human life?

—*Saint Augustine*

A MAN IS STANDING BY THE SIDE OF A TRACK when he sees a runaway train hurtling toward him: clearly the brakes have failed. Ahead are five people, tied to the track. If the man does nothing, the five will be run over and killed. Luckily he is next to a signal switch: turning this switch will send the out-of-control train down a side track, a spur, just ahead of him. Alas, there's a snag: on the spur he spots one person tied to the track: changing direction will inevitably result in this person being killed. What should he do?

From now on this dilemma will be referred to as Spur. Spur is not identical to Winston Churchill's conundrum, of course, but there are similarities. The British government faced a choice. It could do nothing or it could try to change the trajectory of the doodlebugs—through a campaign of misinformation—and so save lives. Different people and fewer people would die as a result. Switching the direction of the train would likewise save lives, though one different person would die as a result.

Figure 1. *Spur.* You're standing by the side of a track when you see a runaway train hurtling toward you: clearly the brakes have failed. Ahead are five people, tied to the track. If you do nothing, the five will be run over and killed. Luckily you are next to a signal switch: turning this switch will send the out-of-control train down a side track, a spur, just ahead of you. Alas, there's a snag: on the spur you spot one person tied to the track: changing direction will inevitably result in this person being killed. What should you do?

Most people seem to believe that not only is it permissible to turn the train down the spur, it is actually required — morally obligatory.

A version of Spur appeared for the first time in the *Oxford Review*, in 1967. The example was later reprinted in a book of essays of which the dedication reads "To The Memory of Iris

Murdoch."[1] It was the author of those essays who had shared a flat with Iris Murdoch during World War II and cowered in the bath at Seaforth Place as the British government was confronted with an analogous problem.[2] Philippa Bonsanquet (later Philippa Foot) could never have guessed that her puzzle, published in a fourteen-page article in an esoteric periodical, would spawn a mini-academic industry and signal the start of a debate that continues to the present day.

It's a debate that draws on the most important moral thinkers in the philosophical canon—from Aquinas to Kant, from Hume to Bentham—and captures fundamental tensions in our moral outlook. To test our moral intuitions, philosophers have come up with ever more surreal scenarios involving runaway trains and often bizarre props: trap doors, giant revolving plates, tractors, and drawbridges. The train is usually racing toward five unfortunates and the reader is presented with various means to rescue them, although at the cost of another life.

The five who are threatened with death are, in most scenarios, innocent: they don't deserve to be in their perilous circumstances. The one person who could be killed to save the five is also, in most scenarios, entirely innocent. There's generally no link between the one and the five: they're not friends or members of the same family: the only connection between them is that they happen to be caught up in the same disastrous situation.

Soon we will meet the Fat Man. The central mystery about how we should treat him has baffled philosophers for nearly half a century. There have now been so many articles linked to the topic that a jokey neologism for it has stuck: "trolleyology."[3]

As an indication of how trolleyology has entered popular consciousness, a version of it was even put to a British prime minister. In front of a live TED audience in July 2009, an interviewer threw Gordon Brown the following curveball. "You're on vacation on a nice beach. Word comes through that there's been a massive earthquake and that a tsunami is advancing on the beach. At one end of the beach there is a house containing a family of five Nigerians. And at the other end of the beach there is a single Brit. You have time to alert just one house. What do you do?" Amidst audience tittering, Mr. Brown, ever the politician, deftly dodged the premise: "Modern communications. Alert both."[4]

But sometimes you can't alert both. Sometimes you can't save everyone. Politicians do have to make decisions that are a matter of life and death. So do health officials. Health resources are not limitless. Whenever a health body is faced with a choice between funding a drug that is estimated to save X lives, and funding another that would save Y, they are, in effect, confronted with a variation of the trolley problem, though these are dilemmas that don't involve killing anybody.[5]

As we'll see, trolleyology has bred subtle and important distinctions: for example, between a choice to save one or to save five on the one hand, and to kill one to save five on the other. At the U.S. Military Academy at West Point, in upper New York State, where future officers come to train, all the cadets are exposed to trolleyology as part of a compulsory course in philosophy and "Just War" theory. It helps underline the difference, the tutors say, between how the United States wages war and the tactics of al-Qaeda: between targeting a military installation knowing that some civilians will inevitably be caught up in the attack and deliberately aiming at civilians.

Philosophers dispute whether or not the trolley scenarios do indeed encapsulate such a distinction. But trolleyology, which was devised by armchair philosophers, is no longer exclusively their preserve. A noticeable trend in philosophy in the past decade is how permeable it has become to the influence and insights from other fields. Nothing illustrates this better than trolleyology. In the past decade this sub-branch of ethics has embraced many disciplines—including psychology, law, linguistics, anthropology, neuroscience, and evolutionary biology. And the most fashionable branch of philosophy, experimental philosophy, has also jumped on the tramwagon. Trolley-related studies have been carried out from Israel to India to Iran.

Some of the trolleyology literature is so fiendishly complex that, in the words of one exasperated philosopher, it "makes the Talmud look like *Cliffs Notes*" (referring to a set of student study guides).[6] Indeed, to an outsider, the curious incidents of the trains on the track may seem like harmless fun—crossword puzzles for long-stay occupants of the Ivory Tower. But at heart, they're about what's right and wrong, and how we should behave. And what could be more important than that?

The Founding Mothers

I realize the tragic significance of the atomic bomb.
—President Harry S. Truman, August 9, 1945,
the day Fat Man is dropped on Nagasaki

PHILIPPA (PIP TO HER FRIENDS) FOOT, the George Stephenson of trolleyology, believed there was a right answer (and so, logically, also a wrong one) to her train dilemma.

Foot was born in 1920 and, like so many of her contemporaries, her ethical outlook was molded by the violence of World War II. But when she began to teach philosophy at Oxford University in 1947, "subjectivism" still had a lingering and, to her mind, pernicious hold on academia.

Subjectivism maintains that there are no objective moral truths. Before World War II it had been given intellectual ballast by a group of mathematicians, logicians, and philosophers from the Austrian capital. They were known as the Vienna Circle. The Vienna Circle developed "logical positivism," which claimed that for a proposition to have meaning it must fulfill one of two criteria. Either it must be true in virtue of the meaning of its terms (e.g., $2 + 2 = 4$ or "All trains are vehicles"), or it must be in principle verifiable through experimentation (e.g., "the moon is made of cheese," or "five men ahead are roped to the track"). All other statements were literally meaningless.

These meaningless propositions would include bald moral assertions, such as "The Nazis were wrong to gas Jews," or "The British were justified in using subterfuge to alter the trajectory of the doodlebugs." On the face of it this is an odd claim: these propositions sound as if they make sense and at least the first seems self-evidently true. They're not like the jumble of words, "Trajectory doodlebugs subterfuge British alter justified," which is patently gibberish. How then ought we to interpret ethical statements? One answer was supplied by the English philosopher A. J. Ayer, who'd attended sessions of the Vienna Circle.[1] Later he would say of logical positivism that "the most important of [its] defects was that nearly all of it was false,"[2] but for a time he was entirely under its spell. Ayer developed what is pejoratively called the boo-hooray theory.[3] If I say, "The Nazis were wrong to gas the Jews," that's best translated as, "The Nazis gassed the Jews: boo, hiss." Likewise, "The British were justified in using subterfuge to alter the trajectory of the doodlebugs" is roughly translatable as "The British used subterfuge to alter the trajectory of the doodlebugs: hoorah, hoorah."

At the onset of Philippa Foot's career, the full horrors perpetrated in the concentration camps of World War II were still being exposed and would haunt her. The notion that ethical claims could be reduced to opinion and to personal preferences, to "I approve," or "I disapprove," to "hooray-boo," was to her anathema.

But not only was Foot radically out of step with ethical emotivism, she also had little time for an alternative approach to philosophy which for a period in the 1950s and 1960s dominated the discipline in Oxford and beyond—"ordinary language" philosophy. The ordinary language movement believed that, before philosophical problems could be resolved, one had to attend to the subtleties of how language is deployed in everyday speech. Philosophers would spend their time deconstructing fine distinctions between our uses of, for example, "by mistake" and "by accident."[4] A student who spoke up in a lecture or tutorial would invariably hear the question boomerang back: "what exactly do you mean when you say XYZ?" Pupils of Foot recall her dutifully teaching this approach, but halfheartedly, and only so that they could pass exams.

Foot was not a natural teacher. She was solicitous, encouraging, but intimidating. She had a long, patrician face and a plummy voice, sounding according to one student "like a Grande Dame."[5] The first impression, that she came from an aristocratic English family, would have captured a half-truth. Her parents were married in Westminster Abbey in one of the social events of the year. Her father, Captain William Sydney Bence Bosanquet, a World War I war hero, was from what Foot herself described as the hunting, fishing, and shooting set. Foot was brought up in an imposing country house and given almost no formal schooling, though she was surrounded by governesses. It was not a culture in which it was deemed advisable or worthwhile to educate girls (Foot's spelling was always atrocious). When to everyone's surprise Pip was offered a place at Oxford to read Politics, Philosophy, and Economics, a friend of the family consoled the parents with the thought that "at least she doesn't look clever."[6]

Foot never objected to intellectual snobbery, but university liberated her from the social snootiness at home. She neither flaunted nor hid her privileged background. Her studies began a month after Britain had declared war on Germany: during the war, while most of the female undergraduates stitched their own skirts out of blackout material, Philippa's clothes were fashionable and always "conspicuously not home-made."[7] She became the focus of particular attention from her economics tutor, Tommy (later Lord) Balogh, a brainy, bullying, and philandering Jewish-Hungarian émigré, who became an adviser to Harold Wilson—an enthralling character though an "emotional fascist."[8] Balogh had many affairs: according to Foot's tutorial partner, Pip endured a sustained courtship campaign, refusing his proposals—made in a thick accent—of marriage.[9]

But only half of Philippa Foot's pedigree was posh-English: her mother could claim more illustrious lineage still. Esther was born in 1893, in the White House. She was the daughter of the twenty-second president and the twenty-fourth president of the United States. This sounds like a logic teaser, since no woman has ever held that office. But the descriptions, "22nd President" and "24th President," have, as philosophers might put it, the same reference. The Democrat, Grover Cleveland, Foot's grandfather, was the only president ever to serve in two nonconsecutive terms.

Foot was fascinated by her grandfather's life (and knew her grandmother reasonably well), but it wasn't the "done" thing to boast about such a connection. In public she was far more likely to refer to a link with a relative on her father's side: Bernard Bosanquet—the cricketer credited with inventing the game's most devious delivery, the googly.

Ménage à quatre

After the war, Philippa Foot persuaded her college, Somerville, then an all-women college, to take on a second philosopher, Elizabeth Anscombe, who has an indirect but vital role in trolleyology. Like Foot, Anscombe never took a PhD: in those days a doctorate was a stigma, a sign that you weren't considered worthy of an immediate academic post. Anscombe had studied Classics [Greats] and received a First Class degree despite, it is said, answering "no" in her viva to the question, "is there any fact about the period you are supposed to have studied which you would like to tell us?"[10] She cut her hair short, smoked cigars, drank tea from the saucer, and wore a monocle and trousers—one pair was leopard skin. She had a mellifluous voice, like a clarinet, which she occasionally deployed to be eyewateringly rude.

For many years Foot and Anscombe were confidantes as well as colleagues, united in a visceral aversion to subjectivism. Former students recall the two Somerville tutors retreating to the common room after lunch, sitting on either side of the fireplace and engaging in protracted philosophical discussions.[11] Foot always said she owed a great deal to Anscombe and thought she was one of the best philosophers of her generation. Respect was mutual: when a young Tony Kenny arrived in town as a graduate, Anscombe told him that Foot was the only Oxford moral philosopher worth heeding.

In the late 1940s it was still rare for women to enter academic philosophy, and Oxford was a bastion of male chauvinism. That one generation could produce not only Anscombe and Foot, but Iris Murdoch too—who with Foot's encouragement had applied for and been offered a job at nearby St. Anne's College—was remarkable. The gifted have a tendency to cluster, so it was less than remarkable that their academic and personal lives were so closely intertwined. There would be falling-outs and falling-ins, demonstrations of loyalty and acts of betrayal, philosophical consensus on some matters and bitter divisions on others. When Pip and Iris were flatmates in

London, one of Murdoch's numerous lovers was M.R.D. Foot. M.R.D. Foot became a distinguished historian of the Special Operations Executive, the clandestine organization that operated behind enemy lines in World War II. But in the war, he himself was a daring agent, parachuting into alien territory. He regarded parachuting as "a tremendous, sensual thrill—nothing but love-making with the right companion can touch it."[12]

The thrill was bound up with the danger. Foot was captured and almost killed in 1944, by which stage Murdoch had ditched him, rather callously, in exchange for Tommy Balogh. Murdoch later grew to hate Balogh, calling him Satan and a "horribly clever Jew."[13] But the episode had left M.R.D. Foot feeling ravaged.[14] Looking back, Murdoch wrote that Philippa "most successfully salvaged what was left after my behavior"[15] by marrying M.R.D. Foot herself, in 1945. The complications from this partner-swapping strained relations between the two women for many years. "Losing you & losing you *in that way* was one of the worst things that ever happened to me,"[16] Murdoch wrote to Foot.

After the war, the Foots settled down to domestic life in north Oxford. It seems to have been a relatively happy arrangement to begin with at least, though M.R.D. Foot was devastated when he wasn't awarded a First Class degree in PPE (Politics, Philosophy, and Economics). Pip broke the news to him, and he spent the rest of his life adding to a list he kept of distinguished people who had suffered a similar calamity. Then in the late fifties, quite unexpectedly to Philippa, and with devastating emotional impact, her marriage broke up. In his memoirs, M.R.D. Foot explains it in two lines. "I remained passionately interested in having children; she turned out not to be able to have any. Feeling a fearsome cad, I walked out on her."[17]

At least it led to a thaw between Foot and Murdoch, so much so that they connected almost every corner of the love quadrangle and had a brief affair themselves. Meanwhile, the relationship between Foot and Anscombe itself grew tense. Foot was an atheist, Anscombe a devout Roman Catholic. This chasm in their worldview would eventually become too vast to be bridged by any shared philosophical interests.

And they did share interests as well as an approach to philosophy. In addition to their common assault on hooray-boo meta-ethics, Anscombe, Foot, and Murdoch were preoccupied with the "virtues." In answer to the question, "How should I behave?" in any particular moral dilemma, one approach emphasizes moral obligations and duties: for example, the duty never to lie. An alternative response, utilitarianism, states that what matters are the consequences of an action, whether for example the action saves the most lives, or produces the most happiness. (Anscombe is credited with introducing the word "consequentialism" into philosophy, for her a term of disdain.) But Foot, Anscombe, and Murdoch were attracted by a third way of thinking, which had been almost entirely abandoned, at least in Oxford. Inspired by the work of Aristotle and Aquinas, they stressed the importance of character.[18] An action was good insofar as it exhibited the behavior of a virtuous person. A truly virtuous person will exhibit many virtues. The virtues include pride, temperance, generosity, bravery, and kindness. Foot was said to prize "honesty" as supreme among the virtues.[19]

Aristotle and Aquinas were not the only points of common reference. A more recent and divisive character was also a powerfully felt presence. Born in Vienna in 1889, Ludwig Wittgenstein died in Cambridge in 1951. His genius, beguiling prose, and mesmerizing charisma combined to make him the most influential philosopher in the Anglo-American world.

Anscombe was the most deeply transformed by the Austrian. During the war she had moved to Cambridge to take up a research fellowship. Wittgenstein spent the war working first as a hospital porter and later a laboratory technician in Newcastle, but he returned to Cambridge to lecture. Anscombe attended these lectures and spent hours in conversation with him: he referred to her, with affection, as "old man." Far too idiosyncratic to be a disciple—Wittgenstein had no shortage of these—Anscombe's work was nonetheless indelibly stamped by his style. When others expressed what they took to be a profound thought, she would ruthlessly expose their latent nonsense for patent nonsense. Arguing with Anscombe was likened to having your skin ripped off.

Like so many of those who came into contact with Wittgenstein, she began to adopt some of his traits, such as disquieting silences as she paused for thought in seminars and tutorials, the vise-like holding of her head with her hands, and the agonized expression during intense philosophical debate. She's even said to have developed a hint of an Austrian accent. Some people detected an inauthenticity in her earnestness, but she certainly took philosophy very seriously. Wittgenstein persuaded many of his most talented students to abandon the discipline: fortunately for philosophy, Elizabeth Anscombe stuck to her vocation, though she told her friend, then plain Tony Kenny, "I don't have a thought in my head that wasn't put there by Wittgenstein". "I sometimes think," added Sir Anthony Kenny, "that I don't have a single thought in my head that wasn't put there by Elizabeth."[20]

Anscombe spread the Wittgensteinian gospel to Foot. During her lifetime Foot published several collections of articles, but only one work conceived as a book, *Natural Goodness*. The opening page begins with Wittgenstein and one of only two talks he delivered in Oxford. As Foot recalled:

> Wittgenstein interrupted a speaker who had realized that he was about to say something that, although it seemed compelling, was clearly ridiculous, and was trying . . . to say something sensible instead. "No," said Wittgenstein. "Say what you *want* to say. Be *crude* and then we shall get on." The suggestion that in doing philosophy one should not try to banish or tidy up a ludicrously crude but troubling thought, but rather give it its day, its week, its month, in court, seems to me very helpful.[21]

Wittgenstein believed that philosophical puzzles were natural, easy to make, and yet arose out of conceptual confusion, and so dissolvable by an analysis of language. The aim of philosophy was "to show the fly the way out of the flybottle."[22] And Foot interpreted this as essentially an oral approach, involving two people in therapeutic talk, one trying to express some deep truth, the other pulling back the veil to expose its shallowness. Perhaps, in those daily postprandial debates at Oxford, she imagined herself acting out the role of trapped fly, with Anscombe helpfully pointing to the exit.

It's not easy to conceive of any aspect of philosophy that would be more alien to Wittgenstein than trolleyology. For one thing, Wittgenstein was skeptical that philosophy had anything to contribute to ethics. More important, the focus on the minutiae of a hypothetical puzzle, endlessly reexamined through a myriad of subtly distinct scenarios, ran quite contrary to his style—which grappled with the most fundamental questions in logic and language. This gives us a clue as to what Foot herself must have thought about the bourgeoning subdiscipline she had inadvertently instigated.

The President's Degree

Our philosophers had something else in common. For them moral philosophy was not merely an abstract exercise, to be confined within the manicured quads and courts of mediaeval universities. It mattered. They engaged with what was happening in the world, and believed they had a duty to do so. It wasn't a special duty that accrued to moral philosophers: it was a general duty that derived from being human.

Foot was one of a small group of people who set up a committee for famine relief back in the 1940s. She had initially responded to a newspaper advertisement seeking volunteers to sort out donations to a charity shop on Broad Street in the center of Oxford. The shop took whatever people could give, and then resold it. In the early days there were gifts of false teeth and a live donkey.[23] Now the organization has grown somewhat. Oxfam operates in around one hundred countries and has fifteen thousand shops.

Politics was conducted, of course, from within the framework of the Cold War, and Foot was active in supporting dissidents and émigrés from eastern Europe, especially from Hungary after the 1956 uprising. In 1975, she and Tony Kenny were invited to lecture in Yugoslavia. They'd heard a rumor that a local philosopher, Mihailo Marcović, had been arrested before their arrival, and drew up a trenchant protest document for distribution, hiding it in their luggage. As they smuggled this contraband through customs, both Brits were anxious about being caught. On this occasion their efforts proved unnecessary—Dr. Marcović was in the welcoming party to greet them.

Anscombe, too, was stirred into action by politics and current affairs. Two examples are relevant here. In 1956 there was a proposal to give Harry S. Truman, the thirty-third president of the United States (1945–1953), an honorary degree at Oxford University. Western Europe had much to be grateful to Truman for. After succeeding Franklin Roosevelt in 1945, he had overseen the final months of World War II. In the years following the end of the war, the Berlin Airlift broke the Soviet blockade on the Western part of this city, while the Marshall Plan pumped vast sums of money into the region to rebuild its shattered economies and NATO was established, providing West European countries with a security umbrella.

The voting on any offer for an honorary doctorate would normally have been a routine affair. However, for Truman, the beautiful seventeenth-century Sheldonian Theatre—where such matters are aired in Oxford—was packed to its cupola. Anscombe wrote that the academics had caught wind of her rebellion and they were "whipped up to vote for the honour." The dons at St. John's were simply told, "The women are up to something in Convocation; we have to go and vote them down."[24] A witness recalled events.[25]

> Miss Anscombe rose and (after duly seeking the VC's permission to speak English) delivered an impassioned speech against the award of an Oxford degree to the "man who pressed the button".of the Bomb.

At the time the *Oxford Mail* reported that Anscombe had caused "a sensation."[26] National newspapers also covered her intervention. Getting carried away with her own rhetoric, Anscombe had asked, "If you do give this honour, what Nero, what Genghis Khan, what Hitler, or what Stalin will not be honoured in the future."

The Americans named the bomb dropped on Hiroshima in August 1945 Little Boy. The bomb detonated on Nagasaki three days later, on August 9, was Fat Man. Together they immediately took between 150,000 and 245,000 lives, and the radiation claimed tens of thousands more in subsequent years. Truman said he had ordered the dropping of the bombs—the only time in history that nuclear weapons have been used—to force Japanese surrender and accelerate the end of the war. Within a week, Emperor Hirohito had announced his country's capitulation.

But, as Anscombe stated, for men to choose to kill the innocent as a means to their ends was always murder. She was puzzled by the common cant about Truman's decision being "courageous." "It may be said that Mr. Truman showed great courage in making the decision," she told the assembled academics, "but I should like to know what he had to lose. I should like to think that he had one thing to lose, and that was the chance of an honorary degree at Oxford."

There are various inaccurate accounts printed about what occurred in the vote. The Oxford University archives make it clear that there was no formal count, but that the proposal to honor Truman was approved by a calling out of *placet* [literally, it pleases] and *non placet* [it does not please]. In fact, at least two other people backed Anscombe[27]—Philippa and her then husband M.R.D. Foot. Philippa shared Anscombe's horror of the bomb: her husband, by contrast, believed that dropping the Hiroshima and Nagasaki bombs had shortened the war, saved countless lives, and was fully justified: he only supported Anscombe out of a sense of personal loyalty.[28] A pamphlet Anscombe later wrote about "Mr. Truman's Degree" is dedicated to those who said "Non placet."

The full reason for Anscombe's fury at Truman's pressing the atomic button revolves around the concept of "intention," discussed in the following chapters. Did Truman intend to kill innocent civilians? And her dissection of intention was key to her views on other moral issues. Although Anscombe had, as it were, bipedal support (two Foots) on her Truman stance, Foot and Anscombe held diametrically opposed views on sexual matters—in particular, contraception and abortion—which would cause a permanent rupture between them: "[Anscombe] was . . . more rigorously Catholic than the Pope," said Foot.[29]

Right through the swinging sixties, the decade of feminist awakening and sexual liberation, Anscombe was vehemently defending the Roman Catholic Church's prohibition of contraception and advocating the rhythm method for sex between married couples. She remonstrated with Foot when Oxfam introduced a policy on birth control in the developing world, tearing up her Oxfam subscription. She bandied about the term "murderer" quite liberally, applying it not just to President Truman but to almost any woman who chose to have an abortion.

The moral status of a fetus aroused fervid disagreement among philosophers, and Foot and Anscombe both wrote philosophical essays on the matter. Of course, to some extent it remains a contentious issue, but in most of the developed world the legal right to have an abortion is now settled. This was not the case when Foot first applied her forensic philosophical skills to the issue. The United States would have to wait until the landmark case of *Roe v. Wade* in 1973 to confirm a woman's right to have an abortion. But in Britain the law liberalizing abortion was passed in parliament in October 1967. This was the same year that Philippa Foot published her article— "The Problem of Abortion and the Doctrine of the Double Effect"—in the *Oxford Review*, which introduced trolleyology to the world.

The Seventh Son of Count Landulf

[The Trolley Problem] a lovely, nasty difficulty.
—*J. J. Thomson*

THE SEVENTH SON OF COUNT LANDULF was born near Naples in the early part of the year 1225. The boy, Thomas, displayed exceptional intellectual gifts. He also showed considerable moral integrity. In his view, two of the highest virtues were fortitude and temperance, qualities he possessed in abundance. To his family's fury he determined to become a Dominican friar rather than the Benedictine monk they had planned. Benedictine monks have little interaction with the world. The Dominicans believed not in living behind secluded cloisters, but in traveling and preaching and spreading the word, surviving on charity. At one stage, in an attempt to thwart Thomas's plan, his elder brothers seized him while he was drinking at a spring, and forcibly took him to a family castle. For two years he was unable to leave. His siblings attempted to break his vow of celibacy by dispatching to his quarters an attractive prostitute. When he saw her, Thomas jumped up, grabbed a poker from the fire, and forced her to retreat from the room.[1]

He eventually escaped his captivity and traveled to Germany to pursue his studies under a gifted Dominican friar, who nurtured Thomas's love and respect for Aristotle. Thomas later taught in many places—in Paris, in Rome, in Naples. Everywhere he went, he of course wore the distinctive white tunic and black cloak of the Dominican Order. Until his death in 1274, he wrote prodigiously: exegeses on Aristotle as well as many original works of extraordinary range and depth.

Half a century later this scion of Landulf would be canonized. To become a saint, a person must perform miracles after his death (to demonstrate that he is present in heaven and capable of coming to the aid of the living). But an indication of God's favorable opinion is to have performed miracles too during life. Thomas wasn't a particularly industrious miracle maker, preferring to write and read. But there were several witnesses to corroborate the following story: in Italy, in the last days of his life, when he'd been refusing food, he suddenly announced that he had a craving for herring. That was unfortunate because herring was nowhere to be found around the Italian coast. But then the fishmonger arrived with his usual batch of sardines and upon opening one of the baskets he found, to everyone's astonishment, that it was full of fresh herrings.

It's a story that has been swallowed by devotees who, to this day, pray at the saint's grave in Toulouse for a cure to their ailments. But even non-Catholics venerate Saint Thomas Aquinas. He is regarded by many Catholics as their faith's preeminent theologian, while secular philosophers acknowledge his seminal contributions in areas ranging from the philosophy of mind to metaphysics and the theory of natural law. His work in moral philosophy remains relevant to us today. In particular, he drew up the principles required for a war to be described as just. And he was the first thinker clearly to adumbrate a powerful doctrine. Intentional killing could never be justified, thought Aquinas. But if a person was threatened, and the only option to save their life was to kill the assailant, well, this killing could be morally permissible, provided the intention was self-preservation, and not the taking of a life. Thus was born the Doctrine of Double Effect—henceforth the DDE.[2]

Not One Effect, but Two

Philippa Foot was a careful intellectual mover. According to Tony Kenny, "She was like a climber who would make sure her footing was sound before taking the next step."[3] Foot was more self-deprecating. She once said, "I'm not clever at all. I'm a dreadfully slow thinker, really. But I do have a good nose for what is important. And even though the best philosophers combine cleverness and depth, I'd prefer a good nose over cleverness any day!"[4]

In 1967, in a seminal article, her philosophical nose led her to one of the most contentious areas in moral philosophy. The full title of the article was "The Problem of Abortion and the Doctrine of Double Effect." In it, Foot rejects the use of the DDE as a weapon to criticize abortion.

She explains the DDE, first identified by Thomas Aquinas, as "based on a distinction between what a man foresees as a result of his voluntary action and what, in the strict sense, he intends."[5] Later she adds, "By 'the doctrine of double effect' I mean the thesis that it is sometimes permissible to bring about by oblique intention what one may not directly intend." It is called the doctrine of *double* effect because of the twin effects of some actions: the one aimed at, the other foreseen but not intended.

A literary example comes from Nicholas Monsarrat's *The Cruel Sea*.[6] The book is set in World War II and the battle of the Atlantic. A British merchant convoy has been struck by German torpedoes. Ships have been sunk and there are many survivors in the sea, waiting to be rescued. The commander of a British corvette is faced with the decision whether to drop a depth charge, to destroy a German U-boat knowing that the massive explosion will kill the survivors. He knows too that if he doesn't take this action, the U-boat will continue to wreak havoc, sinking ship after ship. He drops the depth charge. In making his decision to sink the U-boat, the commander foresaw, but did not intend, the deaths of the survivors.

This distinction between intending and foreseeing is at the core of the DDE. In Catholic theology, the DDE has been pivotal to the church's explanation of why, in its view, there are only rare cases in which abortion is acceptable. Most cases of abortion involve the intentional killing of the fetus. But if a pregnant woman has a tumor in her uterus, and a hysterectomy is required to save her life, the fact that there is also a fetus in the womb is, as it were, incidental. The aim of the hysterectomy is not to kill the fetus (or indeed to have any effect on the fetus) but to deal with the tumor.

The DDE is not just fundamental to Catholicism: it's cited far beyond the pulpit. Some nonbelievers are minded to reject any tenet originating in theology—a puerile stance since so many philosophers have made their contributions from within a religious framework. But the centrality of the DDE in commonsense morality should give theists and nontheists alike at least pause. The DDE is built into law, into medical practice, and into the rules of war. The law draws a distinction between "direct" or "purposeful" intention on the one hand and "oblique" intention on the other. In medicine, it is permitted under certain circumstances to administer a dying person a pill, to reduce her pain, foreseeing but not intending that this

---

The DDE

The DDE can be given a more precise formulation. It's usually seen as consisting of four components, though this formulation is not universally accepted. The DDE comes into play when:

- the act considered independently of its harmful effects is not in itself wrong;
- the agent intends the good and does not intend the harm either as means or end, though the individual may foresee the harm;
- there is no way to achieve the good without causing the harmful effects; and
- the harmful effects are not disproportionately large relative to the good being sought.

The justifiability of targeting a particular military installation illustrates how the DDE can be applied. If it is legitimate to hit an installation with foreseen collateral damage then, according to the DDE, the following conditions must be met: (1) Hitting this installation must not in itself be wrong. (2) Hitting the installation must be the intended act, and the collateral damage must not be intended. (3) It must be impossible to hit the military installation without causing the collateral damage. (4) The badness of the collateral damage must not be disproportionate to the good that will result from hitting the installation.

---

will hasten her death. But it is not permitted to administer a pill intending to bring about her death. It is permitted in certain circumstances to target a military installation in war, foreseeing that it will bring about some civilian casualties (that dreadful euphemism, "collateral damage"); it is not permitted to deliberately target civilians.

Whether or not we're aware of it, the DDE appears to play a role in our daily judgments of approbation and disapproval, from deadly serious instances to more trivial ones. As philosopher Sir Anthony Kenny puts it, "There's surely a difference between appointing A over B for a professorship because A is the best candidate and knowing B will be annoyed, and appointing A over B just to annoy B—I've known both cases."[7] Studies suggest that most people do find the DDE intuitively appealing (see chapter 9).

Not everyone is persuaded. The American philosopher Thomas Scanlon argues that the onus should be on proponents of the DDE to show why we should take it seriously. "[N]o one has . . . come up with a satisfying theoretical explanation of why . . . the difference between consequences that are intended and those that are merely foreseen . . . should make a moral difference."[8] And there's a practical worry that the DDE could be used as an excuse to skip over or shimmy around the taking of responsibility—especially when actions are taken on behalf of a state. Should we be satisfied with the defense minister who orders a highly effective raid against a wicked enemy, but who says, "I realized that villagers would be killed in the bombing: that side-effect of our operation is regrettable"?

Murder at the Hospital

The method of trolleyology involves conjuring up various trolleyesque scenarios and taking note of the (preferably) strong moral intuitions that they elicit. Then he or she tries to formulate a plausible principle (or principles) that unites and makes sense of these intuitions. The principle should itself have some intuitive plausibility: it should not feel arbitrary. Once located, this principle can be transplanted into real life to help resolve real dilemmas.

The DDE is one possible candidate for a principle that explains our intuitions. In exploring the validity of the DDE in her article, Philippa Foot describes several imaginary thought experiments. At the time, the hoariest involved a fat man—but not the fat man who stars as the main protagonist of this book. This earlier fat man is stuck in a hole in a cave. His head is out of the cave, so he can breathe, but a party of potholers is behind him, and unable to escape. "Obviously," wrote Foot, "the right thing to do is to sit down and wait until the fat man grows thin; but philosophers have arranged that flood waters should be rising within the cave."[9] You have a stick of dynamite. The question is; can you use it to blow up the fat man?

It is only on page twenty-three that the trolley is introduced. In fact, in its original form, it differs from the usual description in a few details. Foot asks us to imagine not that the person facing the dilemma is a bystander near the track, but that he is actually driving the train. More trivially, and peculiarly, the vehicle is not a train, but the unthreatening, slow-trundling tram. Trams had largely disappeared from the developing world by the time Foot wrote her article. Among the safest forms of transport ever invented, they were not in the habit of careening out of control, though one of the most celebrated architects of the last two centuries, the Catalan modernist Antoni Gaudi, was knocked down by a tram in Barcelona in 1926 on his way to confession and died a few days later. (In the subsequent inquiry the driver said that he saw a man, who looked like a tramp, cross his path—there had been no time to slow down.) But "tram," not "train," was how Foot conceived her problem, and when it crossed the Atlantic it was Americanized and became a trolley—hence trolleyology. (A rather unfortunate label for British readers, for whom the image is conjured up of marauding supermarket carts full of baked beans and washing powder.)

Foot compares her scenario, which we're calling Spur— where it seems right to turn the trolley (or tram) to save the five even though one will thereby die—with a twin set of cases. These cases run roughly as follows. Imagine we could either save a patient with a massive dose of a drug, or save five patients who only need a fifth each of this drug: what should we do? Once again it would be permissible, thinks Foot, to save the five though one will die. Now take the Transplant Case. Suppose that there are five seriously ill patients, all in urgent need of organ transplants. Two require kidneys, two need lungs, one needs a heart. They will die today unless the organs are forthcoming. As luck would have it, an innocent, healthy, young man who has just the right blood type walks in for his annual checkup: should the surgeon bump him off so that his organs can be farmed out to the five at risk? We are expected to find this proposal abominable.[10]

The fat man, a character we're about to meet, dramatizes much the same conundrum. The question is why our moral reactions differ in these two kinds of cases—cases such as Spur, where it seems morally acceptable to take a life to save five lives, and cases such as Transplant, where it doesn't. One disquieting aspect of these examples is that although most people have instant, powerful, and unyielding reactions to them, they can't usually articulate why they feel so strongly, nor can they easily identify a compelling rationale for the distinction they want to draw.[11]

Yet the DDE appears to provide just such a rationale. After

all, we do not intend to kill the single man in Spur, but we do intend to kill the healthy patient whose organs will save five lives. In Spur, if, after you've switched the train's direction, the man on the track were somehow to untie himself and escape in the nick of time, you would be delighted. Not only would you have avoided crashing into the five, but no one else would have gotten hurt. But with the healthy patient, you require his death—if the visitor's suspicions were aroused when he saw an orderly approach with a bludgeon, any successful escape by him would mean the five would die. His death is a means to save the five.

More about this distinction later. But Foot believed that we do not need to resort to the DDE to explain our intuitions in these scenarios. She proffered an alternative explanation. We have, she says, both negative and positive duties. Negative duties are the duties not to interfere in other people's lives (say by killing them!). Positive duties are duties to help others. In Spur, her dilemma is faced by the driver (not a bystander), and since the driver presumably started the train, his terrible choice is between killing one and killing five, with the former being obviously preferable to the latter. But in the hospital scenario, although the surgeon has a positive duty to save the lives of the five sick patients, this is in conflict and outweighed by the negative duty not to harm a healthy patient.

In a subsequent article Foot went on to highlight what to her was a crucial point. In Spur one is merely redirecting an already existing threat. The runaway train is a moving threat and all we are doing is nudging it, as it were, elsewhere. But in the hospital case, in taking the life of the healthy man, we have introduced a whole new threat.

It's a nice try, but can it be right? Has Philippa Foot solved her own conundrum?

Fat Man, Loop, and Lazy Susan

Always recognize that human individuals are ends,
and do not use them as means to your end.

—*Immanuel Kant*

I am the man, the very fat man,
that watered the workers' beer . . .

— *music hall song*

Don't want to be a fat man,
People would think that I was
Just good fun.
Would rather be a thin man,
I am so glad to go on being one.

—*Ian Anderson, "Fat Man"*
(performed by Jethro Tull)

PHILIPPA FOOT SET TROLLEYOLOGY rolling, but it was Judith
Jarvis Thomson, a philosopher at the Massachusetts Institute
of Technology, who delivered its most high-voltage jolt. Struck
by Foot's thought experiment she responded with not one but
two influential articles on what she labeled "The Trolley
Problem."[1]

The first article included many thought experiments of her own, involving, in order, the imaginary Alfred, Bert, Charles, David, Frank, George, Harry, and Irving, all faced with life-and-death decisions Thus Alfred, who hates his wife, puts cleaning fluid in her coffee, killing her, while Burt, who also hates his wife, sees her putting cleaning fluid in her coffee by mistake (believing it to be cream). Although Burt has the antidote to the cleaning fluid, he does not give it to his wife—he lets her die.

But it was only in the second article that Thomson introduced the stout character who appears in the title of this book.

Foot had originally contrasted the dilemma in Spur with the option of framing an innocent man to save the five hostages and of killing a man so that his organs could save five patients. Thomson made the contrast starker still by introducing another trolley dilemma.

This time you're on a footbridge overlooking the railway track. You see the trolley hurtling along the track and, ahead of it, five people tied to the rails. Can these five be saved? Again, the moral philosopher has cunningly arranged matters so that they can. There's a very fat man leaning over the railing watching the trolley. If you were to push him over the footbridge he would tumble down and smash on to the track below. He's so obese that his bulk would bring the trolley to a juddering halt. Sadly, the process would kill the fat man. But it would save the other five.

Would you kill the fat man? Should you kill the fat man?

The reference to the man's obesity is not gratuitous. If the train could be stopped by anybody of any size, and if you're standing next to the fat man, then presumably the proper action is not to push the fat man, but to leapfrog over the railings

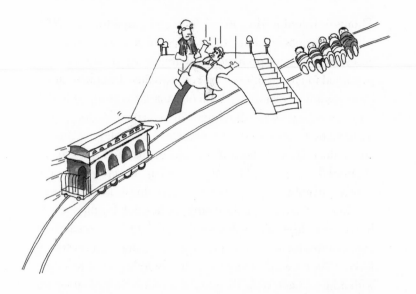

Figure 2. *Fat Man.* You're on a footbridge overlooking the railway track. You see the trolley hurtling along the track and, ahead of it, five people tied to the rails. Can these five be saved? Again, the moral philosopher has cunningly arranged matters so that they can be. There's a very fat man leaning over the railing watching the trolley. If you were to push him over the footbridge, he would tumble down and smash on to the track below. He's so obese that his bulk would bring the trolley to a shuddering halt. Sadly, the process would kill the fat man. But it would save the other five. Should you push the fat man?

and sacrifice yourself. A courageous and selfless act, but in this example, it would be a futile gesture: *ex hypothesi* you are not bulky enough to stop the train.

Even though the man's size is a necessary component of the thought experiment, and even though he is fictional, drawing attention to his scale is considered by some to be indecent.

Thomson introduced us to the fat man in an article in 1985, when academics had long internalized the need to be cautious and sensitive about prejudice and language, particularly as it pertained to race, religion, sex, and sexuality. The obese, however, were not seen as a self-identifying group subject to discrimination and in need of linguistic policing. By 2012, a UK parliamentary body was recommending that calling someone fat be deemed a "hate crime." And in many of the articles about trolleyology, the fat man has undergone a physical, or at least a conceptual, makeover: he has become a "large" man, or a " "heavy" man, or a man of girth. Better still, for those easily hurt, a near-duplicate philosophical problem has been devised that removes the need to allude to the potential victim's corpulence. This time you're standing on a footbridge next to a man with a heavy backpack. Together, the man and his bag would stop the train. Of course, there's no time to unstrap the backpack and jump over the bridge wearing it yourself. The only way to save the five is to push the man with the bag.

However described—and I am going to refer to the fat man with his traditional label—it looks, once again, as though the DDE might help explain the typical moral intuition here: that we can turn the train in Spur but not push the fat man (or man with bag). As previously argued, in Spur you don't want to kill the man on the track. But with Fat Man, you *need* the obese man (or the man with the heavy bag) to come between the trolley and the five at risk. If he were not there, the five would die. He is a means to an end, the end of stopping the trolley before it kills five people. It would be a noble sacrifice if the fat man were to jump of his own accord.[2] But if you push him you are using him as if he were an object, not an autonomous human being.

Like Philippa Foot, however, Thomson was told not to resort to the DDE to explain the difference. She wanted to appeal to the notion of "rights." Like Foot, she was preoccupied with one of the touchstone issues of the day, abortion, and had already appealed to rights theory in her most famous article on the subject, "A Defense of Abortion."[3] This article imagined that you wake up one day lying next to a famous violinist, both of you plugged into a machine. The violinist had had a fatal kidney ailment. On discovering that you alone have the right blood type to help, the Society of Music Lovers hooked the two of you into a contraption so that your kidneys could be used by him as well. Medical staff explain that, regrettably, were the violinist to be unplugged, he would die but, not to worry, this awkwardness will only last nine months, by which time he'll be back to normal and the two of you can go your separate ways. Thomson's claim was that it might be very nice of you to permit the violinist to remain yoked to your body, but he or the hospital would have no *right* to insist that you do so.

Likewise, Thomson appealed to rights in Fat Man. Toppling the fat man is an infringement of his rights. But turning the trolley in Spur is not an infringement of anybody's rights. "It is not morally required of us that we let a burden descend out of the blue onto five when we can make it instead descend onto one."[4] The bystander is not just minimizing the number of deaths by turning the train down the spur; he or she is minimizing "the number of deaths which get caused by something that already threatens people."[5]

Note the similarity to Foot's argument that in Spur one is merely redirecting a preexisting threat, whereas pushing the poor fat man introduces a completely new threat. This distinction feels plausible: it feels as if it should carry some moral

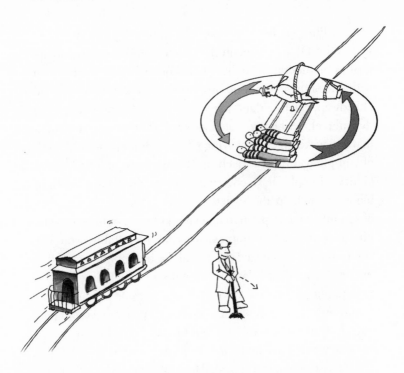

Figure 3. *Lazy Susan.* In Lazy Susan you can save the five by twisting the revolving plate 180 degrees—this will have the unfortunate consequence of placing one man directly in the path of the train. Should you rotate the Lazy Susan?

weight. But one trolleyologist[6] insists it does not. She offers, as evidence, Lazy Susan.[7]

In Lazy Susan, you can save the five by twisting the revolving plate 180 degrees—this will have the consequence of placing one man directly in the path of the train. Nonetheless, says the inventor of this scenario, it's permissible to turn the lazy susan—even though this is not about diverting an existing

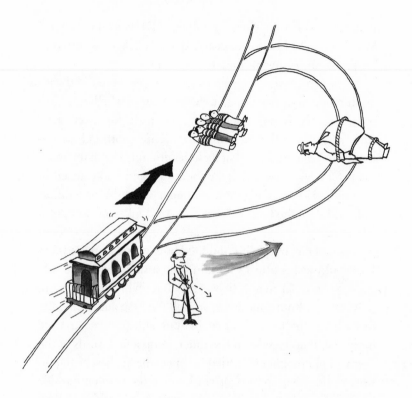

Figure 4. *Loop.* The trolley is heading toward five men who, as it happens, are all skinny. If the trolley were to collide into them they would die, but their combined bulk would stop the train. You could instead turn the trolley onto a loop. One fat man is tied onto the loop. His weight alone will stop the trolley, preventing it from continuing around the loop and killing the five. Should you turn the trolley down the loop?

threat; for the individual who will die, it introduces an entirely new threat.

You may not share that intuition. If you do, the search for a principle to explain our other intuitions in Fat Man and Spur continues. But what's wrong with the DDE as the answer? Why wouldn't Thomson appeal to that? Well, because of a trolley problem she invents that we can call Loop.

A number of weeks have passed since you were faced with an instant and excruciating choice in Spur of whether to turn the train down the side track. Then, you made the correct decision: you turned the train. In the interim, workers have extended the side track, so that it circles around back to the main track. Once again you've gone for a walk and find yourself in the midst of a similar nightmare, though with a slight modification. In Loop, the train is heading toward five men who, as it happens, are all skinny. If the train were to collide into them they would die, but their combined bulk would stop the train. You could instead turn the train onto a side track. The side track has one fat man. His weight alone will stop the train, preventing it from continuing around the loop and killing the five. There's this key difference. In Spur, if the single man were to escape, that would—in the much lampooned words of the German philosopher Gottfried Leibniz—be the best of all possible worlds.[8] Not so in Loop. In Loop, if the man on the side track were to disappear, the five skinny men would be killed: this time you need his death to save the five. The collision with this man is therefore surely part of your plan.

Nonetheless, writes Thomson, given that we agree that it would be acceptable, if not obligatory, to turn the train in Spur, it must be equally acceptable to do so in Loop, for, as she puts it, "we cannot really suppose that the presence or absence of that extra bit of track makes a major moral difference as to what an agent may do in these cases."[9]

If Thomson is right, the DDE cannot be the principle to justify a distinction between Spur and Fat Man.[10] For in Loop we don't merely foresee the fat man's death: we need the fat man to die—we intend his death. Turning the trolley in Loop falls foul of the DDE.

So it looks as if we've hit the buffers again. We have identified a common intuition that it is sometimes wrong to take a life even though five lives would be saved. Can we ground this intuition in principle? The attempt to do that takes us back to the eighteenth century and the remote Prussian outpost of Königsberg.

Ticking Clocks and the Sage of Königsberg

*Out of the crooked timber of humanity
no straight thing was ever made.*

—*Immanuel Kant*

AN ELEVEN-YEAR-OLD BOY has been kidnapped. He was last seen getting off the Number 35 bus on his way home on the final school day before the autumn holiday. He's now been missing for three days and is considered to be in mortal danger. The police have arrested the chief suspect. He was captured after picking up a ransom of one million Euros. The ransom had been demanded in a note left on the gate of the boy's home — and had been dropped, as agreed, at a trolley stop on a Sunday night. Instead of releasing the boy, the man went on a spending spree with his million Euros. He booked a foreign holiday; he ordered a C-class Mercedes.

The police are as certain as they can be that they have the guilty man — a tall, powerfully built law student, who'd previously been employed to give the boy extra tutoring. Now they urgently need to locate the boy. They don't know how long they have to save his life: is he locked away in a cellar, without access to water and food? The interrogation of the law student begins: the clock ticks—and ticks, and ticks, and ticks. A search involving 1,000 police, helicopters, and tracker dogs yields nothing. And, after seven hours of questioning, the suspect has still not given up the boy's whereabouts.

The police officer in charge writes down an instruction to the interrogators: they are to threaten to torture the suspect. "A specialist" will be flown in, they tell the suspect, whose function it will be to inflict unimaginable pain until they extract the information they need.

The suspect cracks. He reveals where the boy is being held.

An Icy Gust

This kidnapping occurred in Germany in 2002. The kidnapper was Magnus Gäfgen, a law student in his mid-twenties. The victim, Jakob von Metzler, was the heir to a fortune: his father ran Germany's oldest family-owned bank.

The story does not have a happy ending. Frightened, under pressure, faced with a horrifying ordeal, Gäfgen told the police that Jakob could be found at a lake near Frankfurt. When they arrived, they discovered the boy's body: he'd already been killed, and was in a sack, wrapped in plastic and still dressed in the blue top and sand-colored trousers in which he'd last been spotted.

The case became a *cause célèbre*, not just because Jakob came from a prominent family, but more especially after allegations surfaced of the torture threat. Frankfurt's deputy police chief, Wolfgang Daschner, who had written the "torture" note, gave various interviews to the press. He'd faced a stark choice, he said. "I can just sit on my hands and wait until maybe Gäfgen eventually decides to tell the truth and in the meantime the child is dead, or I do everything I can now to prevent that from happening."[1]

The torture threat, apparently, had not been an idle one. A martial arts trainer had been put on call: the police believed the suspect could be hurt without lasting physical damage being inflicted upon him.

There were expressions of outrage at Daschner's behavior. One MP from the Green Party warned that, "if you open the window, even just a crack, the cold air of the Middle Ages will fill the whole room."[2] But Daschner also had vocal supporters, and polls showed that the majority of Germans believed the threat was a reasonable means of potentially saving a life. When, in court, Gäfgen's lawyer attempted to use the torture threat to have the case dismissed, spectators were heard to grumble, "Incredible: How many rights does he want for this guy?"[3] And amidst the uproar from human rights groups, Daschner commented, "Not one single person has been able to tell me what I should have done."[4]

No-harm Zone

There could be no trolleyology without deontology.

Deontology states that there are certain things, like torture, that you just shouldn't do. We mustn't take an entirely impersonal perspective on morality. An individual's well-being shouldn't just be stirred and dissolved into some giant vat of well-being soup. We can't torture someone to death even if this would save five lives—even if it would, in the utilitarian sense, contribute to the total sum of happiness. Some deontologists are absolutists—for them, nothing could ever justify torture. But most accept that in certain circumstances deontological constraints can be overridden, for example if the future of the planet is at stake.

Central to the history of deontology was an eighteenth-century professor, the guru of Königsberg (a city then in East Prussia, now a Russian enclave renamed Kaliningrad), Immanuel Kant. Kant made major contributions in numerous areas of philosophy, not just ethics. He is among the greatest metaphysicians of all time—preoccupied with the limits of what we can know and understand about reality.

Given his significance one might expect library shelves to groan under weighty biographies of his life. In fact there are few such tomes, explained by the fact that Kant lived an exceptionally regular and uneventful life. He attended the University of Königsberg and later taught there. There is virtually no account of his life in Königsberg that doesn't include the possibly apocryphal story that the citizens of the city used to set their watches by his movements—he would take a daily walk at 4:30 p.m. and go up and down the street eight times. The one time he was late (another possibly apocryphal story has it) was when he received a copy of Rousseau's tract on education, *Émile*, and was so enthralled and absorbed by it that he lost all track of time.

In Kant's view, persons must never be treated merely as a means to some other end. This was expressed most clearly in one formulation (there are several) of his "Categorical Imperative." The Categorical Imperative is an absolute moral requirement for all times, all situations, all circumstances, and from which all other duties and obligations follow. Kant believed the Categorical Imperative could be derived through the exercise of our reason alone. The relevant version of his Categorical Imperative—the second formulation—asserts that we should always treat others "never merely as a means to an end, but always at the same time as an end."

It's a simple idea to state, though it's hard to work out what it entails in particular cases, both real and imaginary. However, its influence has been pervasive: the modern human rights movement is almost inconceivable without Kant. (In surely its most ironic use, the Nazi war criminal, Adolf Eichmann, who was responsible for organizing the mass deportation of Jews to the concentration camps, justified himself during his trial in Jerusalem in 1961 by citing Kant's Categorical Imperative.)[5]

One of those who has tried to set out in more detail what it means for humans to be enveloped in a moral carapace, a protective shield that is both sacred and inviolable, is Philippa Foot.

> The existence of a morality which refuses to sanction the automatic sacrifice of the one for the good of the many . . . secures to each individual a kind of moral space, a space which others are not *allowed* to invade. Nor is it impossible to see the rationale of the principle that one man should not want evil, serious evil, to come on another, even to spare *more* people the same loss. It seems to define a kind of solidarity between human beings, as if there is some sense in which no one is to *come out against* one of his fellow men.[6]

If there are certain moral absolutes—rules that tell us certain actions are always wrong and can never be sanctioned—then one of them, surely, is the prohibition on torture.

Clocks and Clichés

Browse through one section of the moral philosophy literature and you'll hear a cacophony of ticking clocks. The ticking-clock scenario is a favorite among ethicists debating the permissibility, or otherwise, of torture. A terrorist has been captured: you know that he has planted a small atomic bomb in a major city that is due to detonate in two hours. The terrorist will not tell you where the bomb is, and unless you use torture to obtain the information from him, thousands of people will die. What should you do?

Post–9/11, when it became evident that there were people in the world bent on the goal of mass civilian murder, the ticking bomb of ethical debate took on a practical and public reality. A distinguished law professor, Alan Dershowitz, scandalized liberal opinion by writing a book in which he proposed the idea of a "torture warrant" that would be given to interrogators by governments in certain extreme circumstances.[7] Since then there have been well-publicized torture scandals, such as the waterboarding of al-Qaeda operative, Khalid Sheikh Mohammed, thought to be a mastermind behind the 9/11 atrocities.

In response to the ticking-bomb case, deontologists respond in one of five ways.

First, there are those who deny that the ticking bomb reflects any possible empirical reality. In reality, threats are not usually imminent: there is no specific deadline, nor is the threat inevitable. In reality, we couldn't know for sure that lives would be lost. What's more, torture may prove ineffective or, worse, counterproductive—producing false confessions. And there may be alternative and legitimate ways to extract reliable information or in some other way resolve the crisis.[8]

Second, some deontologists are prepared to swallow the logical conclusion of an absolutist position—they continue to deny the permissibility of torture, regardless of how many lives would be saved.

Third—and this is perhaps the standard view—there are deontologists who argue that if the consequences of not torturing somebody are truly calamitous (leading, for example, to the deaths of thousands), then the constraint against torture can be overridden.

Fourth, a few deontologists maintain that a terrorist who has planted a ticking bomb is morally liable to be tortured if that's the only way to obtain vital information. In other words, there is no constraint on torturing this person. It's not that the potential consequences of the explosion outweigh any constraint; rather, the terrorist has, by his actions, forfeited his right not to be tortured, and his torture is acceptable even if the bomb for which he's responsible threatened only one life.[9]

Fifth, there are those who determinedly refuse to engage with the scenario, who believe the justifiability of torture should not be up for discussion at all: merely to raise the possibility reflects a sickness of the mind, and a contamination of the culture. As one philosopher puts it: "Society is to some degree defined by what is undiscussable in it. For example, in our society, it's undiscussable whether we should enslave our black population . . . the things we find undiscussable are things that we treat as having no two sides."[10] Torture is one such subject, it is said: a subject with only one side.

The Gäfgen kidnapping was about as close to the ticking-bomb cliché as real life gets, though even here the parallels are far from exact: since, as it turned out, torturing the kidnapper would have been futile. Jakob had already been killed, and thus there was no life to save. But, nonetheless, it nicely illustrates the clash between deontological and consequentialist ethics.

That clash is a common trope in literature. Euripides' play, *Iphigenia in Aulis*, revolves around Agamemnon's decision whether to sacrifice his eldest daughter, Iphigenia. If he does so, the goddess Artemis will stop meddling with the elements and release the wind that is holding Agamemnon's fleet in harbor, thus allowing Agamemnon's troops to sail against the archenemy Troy and ending the threat of their mutiny. (Iphigenia eventually resolves the dilemma by sacrificing herself.)

In *The Brothers Karamazov*, Dostoyevsky puts these words into his character Ivan, speaking to his brother:

> Tell me straight out, I call on you—answer me: imagine that you yourself are building the edifice of human destiny with the object of making people happy in the finale, of giving them peace and rest at last, but for that you must inevitably and unavoidably torture just one tiny creature, [one child], and raise your edifice on the foundation of her unrequited tears—would you agree to be the architect on such conditions?[11]

The trolley problem speaks to such dilemmas. The Doctrine of Double Effect cited in trolleyology is clearly, in the jargon, nonconsequentialist, since it claims a distinction can be drawn between two acts that have identical consequences. And the DDE has several deontological siblings. Many philosophers claim that there is a distinction between negative and positive duties, between doing and allowing (killing and letting die), and between acting and omitting. Thus, Philippa Foot claims that failing to save a life by not donating to charity is not nearly as bad as actually taking a life: "We are not inclined to think that it would be no worse to murder to get money for some comfort such as a nice winter coat than it is to keep the money back before sending a donation to Oxfam or Care."[12]

Those who reject such distinctions tend to adopt the following strategy to discredit them. They describe a pair of cases in which the relevant distinction applies, but that are otherwise identical, and that no right-minded person could believe differ in any morally significant way.

Thus, take the distinction between acts and omissions. We are told that some acts are worse than some omissions. Purportedly it is worse to kill than to fail to save a life. But now imagine that two men, Smith and Jones, both stand to make a fortune if their nephew dies. Smith sneaks into his bathroom one night when his nephew is taking a bath and drowns him, making it look like an accident. In the alternative case, Jones sneaks into the bathroom: he's about to drown him when the boy slips, hits his head, and drowns on his own. Jones watches him die. It doesn't look as if there's a moral distinction between Smith and Jones, even though Smith acts whereas Jones merely fails to act (lets die). And we can thus conclude, runs the argument, that there is no fundamental moral difference between acts and omissions.[13]

Such examples have been seen as a powerful attack on the act-omission and related distinctions. And if the attack succeeds, it has profound repercussions: it makes us, as the moral philosopher Peter Singer believes, as guilty for knowingly failing to save life as for actually taking life. But those who want to maintain that such distinctions have moral force have a crafty response. Just because the distinction is *sometimes* irrelevant, they say, it doesn't mean it's *always* irrelevant. Even if we accept that Smith and Jones are equally culpable, that doesn't prove that all acts are morally equivalent, other things being equal, to all omissions.

This defense is taken up by American philosopher Frances Kamm.[14] The puzzle, then, is to determine when a distinction carries weight, and when it doesn't—and that demands an explanation as to why the distinction is morally significant in some cases but not others.

View through the Kamm-corder

History's best-known trolley victim, the Catalan architect Antoni Gaudí, is celebrated for his ornate, neogothic/baroque designs.

His unfinished masterpiece, the *Sagrada Familia*, draws millions of tourists with its weird, somewhat threatening spires like bejeweled cruise missiles. If there's a philosopher whose style most resembles Gaudí's, it's Frances Kamm. A night creature, she toils away into the early hours devising thought experiments. "I feel that I've been admitted to a whole world of distinctions that haven't been seen by others or at least not by me. And I'm taken by it as I would be by a beautiful picture."[15]

In the search for a formulation of the principles that should govern how we can and can't treat people, Kamm offers (and critiques) some bafflingly baroque principles. Layer of complexity is heaped upon layer. There are principles galore. There is the principle of alternate reason, the principle of contextual interaction, the principle of ethical integrity, the principle of instrumental rationality, the principle of irrelevant goods, the principle of irrelevant need, the principle of irrelevant rights, and the principle of Secondary Wrong. And we should not forget the principle of the Independence of Irrelevant Alternatives of Permissible Harm, or the principle of Secondary Permissibility. The latter two are sufficiently significant to merit their own acronym, the PPH and the PSP.

There's also a smorgasbord of doctrines. However, among them, one is worth highlighting, because it illustrates the ingenuity of Kamm's work, the fine and subtle distinctions she draws, and also because this distinction, at least, has powerful intuitive appeal. She calls it the Doctrine of Triple Effect. It has a third distinction in addition to the two that are familiar from the DDE, namely effects that are intended and effects that are foreseen. She explains it through what she calls the Party Case.

Suppose that I want to give a party, so that people have a good time, though I realize that a party would result in a terrible mess: there would be glasses to wash, carpets to vacuum, and wine stains to scrub off. I foresee that if my friends have fun, they will feel indebted to me (not a nice feeling) and so help me clean up. I decide to hold the party but only *because* I foresee that they'll help me afterward. But I don't hold the party *in order* to make my friends feel indebted, and thus help me: this is not part of my goal. My reason for holding the party is so guests have fun.[16] Kamm draws the conclusion that I don't intend that my guests feel indebted. Similarly, says Kamm, there's a distinction between doing something *because it will cause* the hitting of a bystander, and doing it *intending to cause* the hitting of a bystander.

This pretty distinction can assist in various trolley scenarios.[17] Take the Six Behind One case.

The bystander's predicament is almost exactly as in Spur, with this difference. Behind the one person on the spur are six people, tied to the track. The one person, if hit, will block the trolley. Since it is permissible to turn the trolley in Spur, a natural intuition is that it must be equally permissible to do so in

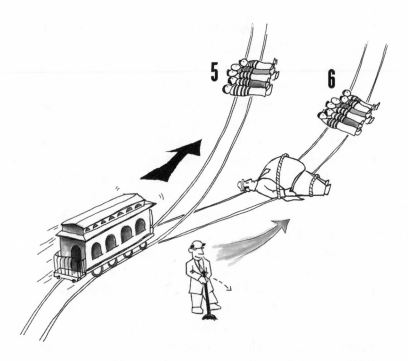

Figure 5. *Six Behind One.* You are standing on the side of the track. A runaway trolley is hurtling toward you. Ahead are five people, tied to the track. If you do nothing, the five will be run over and killed. Luckily you are next to a signal switch: turning this switch will send the out-of-control trolley down a side track, a spur, just ahead of you. On the spur you see one person tied to the track: changing direction will inevitably result in this person being killed. Behind the one person are six people, also tied to the track. The one person, if hit, will stop the trolley. What should you do? This example is from Otsuka 2008.

Six Behind One. But in Spur, the decision to turn the train was justified on the grounds that there was no intention to kill the one. As evidence for this we can imagine how we would feel if this person managed to escape: relief and joy. It would be the best of all possible worlds. The trolley would have been diverted from the five, and no one else would have been killed.

But we can't say the same of Six Behind One. In Six Behind One we want and need the trolley to hit the one. If it doesn't do so, if the one escapes, the trolley will roll on to kill six. There would be no point turning the trolley unless it hit this one.

So does that mean that if we turn the trolley in Six Behind One, we *intend* to kill the one? And are we thus to deduce that turning the trolley in Six Behind One is morally unacceptable? That doesn't seem right, not least because hitting the one is not used as a means to saving the five. We didn't turn the trolley so that we can hit the one.

It's here that Kamm's distinction trundles to the rescue. I can say about the Six Behind One case that if I turn the trolley, I do so not *in order to* hit the one, but *because* it will hit the one—and that's what makes it alright.

As with so many of the scenarios, intuitions about the Six Behind One case will hinge on what the intention is in turning the trolley. Perhaps, then, we should try to clarify what we mean by intention. And we can illustrate the difficulties with a genuine train problem that beset Philippa Foot's most illustrious relation.

Paving the Road to Hell

What is left over if I subtract the fact that my arm
goes up from the fact that I raise my arm?

—*Ludwig Wittgenstein*

Even a dog knows the difference between
being kicked and being stumbled over.

– *Oliver Wendell Holmes, Sr.*

IN MID-1894, GROVER CLEVELAND had personal and public pre-
occupations on his mind. There was concern about his health
and suspicion that he had a malignant tumor. More happily,
his family was expanding. His young wife had eight months
earlier given birth to a second child, Esther, the only presidential child to this day to be born in the White House itself (Esther would eventually move to England, where her daughter
Philippa, would grow up). Meanwhile, seven hundred miles
away, in Chicago, the president had a looming and very public
trolley problem: an industrial relations crisis that threatened
the economic and social stability of the nation.

It had been a boom period for the railroads—Chicago was
the railroad capital of the United States, the Pullman Palace

Car Company was about the most prosperous company in the land, and George Pullman, its austere founder, was one of America's wealthiest citizens. Pullman was an architect of our modern rail system. He built sleeping cars, renowned for their sleek design and opulence. Some of his trains offered exquisite food prepared by revered chefs, and there was attentive service from staff, many of them freed slaves (in the post–Civil War period, Pullman became the largest employer of African Americans). Traveling in a Pullman car was considered the height of luxury.

Working for Pullman was less of a privilege. His rail company had an undeserved reputation for compassionate paternalism. In order to house his thousands of employees, George Pullman came up with the notion of building a model city (one that, today, you can visit and tour), just south of Chicago. The city had all the amenities Pullman deemed necessary—parks, shops, a kindergarten, a library—and he was hailed nationwide as a tremendous benefactor and visionary. He himself said he loved the town like one of his children, and there were a few things to be said in its favor: decent health facilities, for example. But behind the façade, the truth was nastier. Some of the houses were no better than shacks, and often overcrowded: poverty was rife. Pullman ran the place like a despot and not a nickel was donated in charity. The town was expected to pay its way; there were rents and fees for all services (including for use of the library). The one small bar charged inflated prices to deter laborers from frequenting it. The inhabitants were not consulted about what they might want and dissenting views were discouraged: there were no town hall meetings. Leases could be terminated on short notice and tenants might find themselves with nowhere else to go in Pullman, and thus effectively expelled from the tycoon's utopia.

When, in 1883, the U.S. national economy went into a dramatic downturn, the Pullman Company was itself inevitably and acutely affected. Many workers were laid off. Those that held onto their jobs had their wages cut drastically, while rent for their accommodation, which was deducted automatically from their paychecks, remained unchanged. In May 1884, some workers formed a committee and asked the company to lower the rent. A flat refusal sparked wildcat strikes which gathered momentum and escalated the following month into looting, burning, and mob violence. It represented a furious showdown between capital and labor, between the railway industry and the strongest union in the country, the American Railway Union. President Cleveland called it a "convulsion."[1] It was the defining episode of his presidency.

When union members began to boycott Pullman trains, rail networks in Illinois and beyond were paralyzed. The industrial unrest eventually enveloped twenty-seven states. In a highly contentious move—against the wishes of the Illinois governor and resented by many Americans—President Cleveland declared the strike a federal crime and sent in thousands of federal troops. (This would receive legal *ex post facto* vindication in the Supreme Court.) The White House believed that the strike endangered interstate commerce as well as the movement of federal mail. Cleveland swore that if it took "every dollar in the Treasury and every soldier in the United States Army to deliver a postal card in Chicago, that postal card shall be delivered."[2]

The intervention of federal troops served only to enrage the strikers, who almost immediately began to overturn and set alight train carriages, even to attack the troops. President Cleveland issued a proclamation in which he explained that those who continued to resist authority would be regarded as public enemies. The troops had authority "to act with all the moderation and forbearance consistent with the accomplishment of the desired end."[3] But soldiers would be unable, warned Cleveland, to discriminate between the guilty and those who were present at trouble spots from idle curiosity.

Federal troops were reinforced by far less disciplined state troops and marshals. The violence peaked in early June. By the time the strike was over, at least a dozen lives had been lost in the Chicago area and forty more in clashes with troops in other states. A three-man commission quickly produced a 681-page report to examine who was at fault, and what lessons could be learned.

Proving intent does not require a smoking gun.
—New York Times, *August 25, 1912*

Intention is everywhere in the law—not just in criminal law (where it's needed to separate, for example, murder from manslaughter), but in every variety of the law: in tax law, antidiscrimination law, contract law, and constitutional law.

That troops killed rioters in the Pullman strike is beyond doubt. What's more difficult to ascertain is their intention. Did they *intend* to kill? How would we determine whether they did or didn't?

There's a story about Elizabeth Anscombe repeated by so many people who knew her that it's almost certainly false. She was in Montreal, at supper time, and she arrived at an expensive restaurant where she was planning to eat. "Sorry Madam," said the maître d'hôtel, "women are not permitted to wear trousers here." "Give me a minute," said Anscombe. And she disappeared to the rest room to reappear a couple of minutes later with exactly the same outfit, minus the trousers.

It seems unlikely that this is what the concierge intended. In everyday conversation we rarely have trouble understanding what is meant by "intending" or "intention." "Elizabeth Anscombe walked to the shops intending to buy a pint of milk," would not typically invite the riposte, "what do you mean, intending?" It seems obvious. Question: why did Anscombe go to the shops? Answer: to buy some milk. In fact, intention is a notion wrapped in multilayered complications, which Anscombe herself stripped away in her seminal work *Intention.*[4] An intention is not the same as a cause. If someone asks "why did you jump in front of the trolley?" a response might be, "I didn't jump. I was pushed." If an act is intentional it makes sense, said Anscombe, not just to ask "why?" but to expect any answer to explain the action's significance for the person who undertook it.

One of her motives for focusing so much intellectual energy on the concept was her need for a clear understanding of its use in the Doctrine of Double Effect, and in all the ways she applied the DDE, whether in debates over the atomic bomb, abortion, or the use of contraceptives. For example, she believed intention justified distinguishing contraceptive intercourse from intercourse with the rhythm method. The former, but not the latter, she argued, is intended to be nonprocreative, and is immoral. Any sexual act that could never lead to procreation, such as gay sex, was to be condemned. "If contraceptive intercourse is permissible, then what objection could there be after all to mutual masturbation, or copulation *in vase indebito*, sodomy, buggery?"[5]

Anscombe set about minutely dissecting the ways we use intentionality in language: for example as an adverb ("the man is pushing intentionally"), a noun ("the man is pushing the fat man with the intention of toppling him over the bridge"), and verb ("the man intends to push the fat man"). Most of Anscombe's complications need not concern us, but she was the first to point out that an action can be intentional under one description yet not under another. The action of the person who sends the fat man hurtling off the bridge can be intentional under the description "pushing the fat man," but not under the description "stretching his triceps." Of course, the pusher of the fat man does stretch his triceps, but it would sound peculiar to say that he *intended* to do so. If you asked him for an explanation of his action he would be unlikely to respond, "I did it to stretch my triceps."

So did soldiers mean to kill the Pullman rioters? No soldier was ever held responsible for doing so. The tone of the commission report is hardly sympathetic to the victims. The mobs that took possession of the railroad yards and tracks were, it states, "composed generally of hoodlums, women, a low class of foreigners and recruits from the criminal classes."[6] Those hauled in to give testimony to the commission describe the troops as meaning to "protect property," or meaning to "preserve the law." No doubt that is how the individual soldiers would have responded if asked why they used their weapons: "I meant to keep the peace," "I intended to stop the riot," "I meant to prevent interference in interstate trade." But how can you fire into a crowd and not intend to kill? Did they merely intend to wound? Was the killing foreseen but not intended?

There is a deep problem here, which Cleveland's granddaughter, Philippa Foot, raises in her original trolley article. She calls it the problem of "closeness"—and refers to the cave case. Recall that in the cave the waters are rising, the fat man is blocking your escape, and you have a stick of dynamite that would clear a route for you and others but obviously end the fat man's life. Suppose you used this dynamite and afterward declared in court that you'd had no intention of killing the fat man, merely of blowing him into a thousand small pieces. That, says Foot, would be "ridiculous."[7] Blowing a man into a thousand pieces and killing him are one and the same: drawing a distinction between them would be risible. But then we require an account of "closeness" to ensure that such excuses are indeed laughed out of court—and it has proved notoriously tricky to provide one. After all, if talented surgeons were to arrive on the scene and declare that they could somehow stitch the fat man back together, you would be delighted. So it must be true, in this strange sense, that you really don't want the fat man to die.

This is similar to the situation in Loop. It could be said that in turning the train we don't strictly speaking intend to kill the man on the loop. Our intention is merely that he be hit and that the train stop: if the train came to a halt after contact with the man, but he miraculously survived, and then wandered off without so much as a sprained thumb, we wouldn't chase after him with a club in order to beat him to death. We wanted the man to obstruct the train, not to die.

However, as Philippa Foot points out, in practice being hit by a train is a death sentence: to draw a distinction between colliding with and killing a person feels sophistical.

Extra Push

Putting aside the problem of closeness, intentionality, as we've seen, can draw a distinction between Spur and Loop. In *The View from Nowhere*, Thomas Nagel describes certain types of

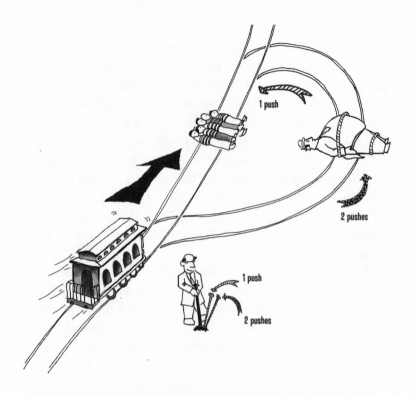

Figure 6. *Extra Push*. The trolley is heading toward the five men who will die if you do nothing. You can turn the trolley onto a loop away from the five men. On this loop is a single man. But the trolley is traveling at such a pace that it would jump over the one man on the side track unless given an extra push. If it jumped over this man, it would loop back and kill the five. The only way to guarantee that it crashes into the man is to give it an extra push. Should you turn the trolley, and should you also give it the extra push?

action as being "guided by evil."[8] One way to make sense of this is to think counterfactually—about "what ifs." What if the man on the Loop were to run away, for example? Nagel writes that if one is guided by an evil goal, "action aimed at it must

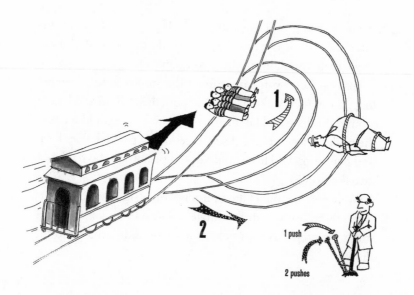

Figure 7. *Two Loop.* The trolley is heading toward five men who will die if you do nothing. You can redirect the trolley onto an empty loop. If you took no further action, the trolley would rattle around this loop and kill the five. However, you could redirect the trolley a second time down a second loop that does have one person on it. This would kill the person on the track but save the five lives. Should you redirect the trolley, not once, but twice?

follow it and be prepared to adjust its pursuit if deflected by altered circumstances."[9]

The "what if" question helps us think about intentionality. For example, take the Extra Push[10] case.

In Extra Push, you can turn the train onto the loop away from the five men, but the train is traveling at such a pace that it would jump over the one man on the side track unless given an extra push. If it jumped over this man, it would loop back and kill the five. The only way to guarantee that it crashes into the man is to give it this extra push. If you give the train this extra push, it seems clear that you would be aiming to hit the single man. Similarly, in the Two Loop case.

In Two Loop you can redirect the trolley onto an empty loop. If you then took no further action, the trolley would rattle around this loop and kill the five. However, you could redirect the trolley a second time down a second loop which does have one person on it. This would kill the person on the track but save the five lives.

Were you to redirect the trolley not once, but twice, to guarantee its collision with the single man on the track, it would surely be preposterous to claim that you didn't *intend* to hit him.[11]

The Knobe Effect

There is one final complication with the concept of intention, unearthed by a new philosophical movement, called "experimental philosophy" or "x-phi" for short, of which more soon. If we're trying to work out whether somebody *intended* to produce a particular effect, we might think that essentially all we needed to do was establish that person's mental state, what the person wanted or believed. But a young philosopher and psychologist, Joshua Knobe, asked subjects about the following two cases—and came up with a surprising result, now known as the Knobe Effect.

- CASE 1: A vice president of a company goes to the chairman of a board and says, "We've got a new project. It's going to make oodles of money for our company, but it's also going to harm the environment." The chairman of the board says, "I realize the project's going to harm the environment. I don't care at all about that. All I care about is making as much money as possible. So start the project." The project starts, and sure enough, the environment suffers.

- CASE 2: A vice president of a company goes to the chairman of a board and says, "We've got a new project. It's going to make oodles of money for our company. It's also going to have a beneficial impact on the environment." The chairman of the board says, "I realize the project's going to benefit the environment. I don't care at all about that. All I care about is making as much money as possible. So start the project." The project starts, and sure enough, there is a beneficial impact on the environment.

The question subjects were asked was whether in each case the chairman *intended* the effect on the environment. And here's the curious part. When asked about the first scenario, most people say "yes, the harm was intentional." But did the chairman in the second scenario intentionally help the environment in the second scenario? Most people thought not.

This is odd, since the two cases seem almost identical. The only difference is that in the first case the chairman has done something bad, and in the second case he has done something good. Knobe believes this shows that the concept of intention is inextricably bound up with moral judgments. More generally, he maintains that such results suggest we should radically rethink how we regard ourselves. We do not function like the ideal scientist, who tries to make sense of the world from an entirely detached perspective. Instead, our way of understanding what goes on is "suffused with moral consideration"[1]: we see the world through a moral lens.

If after all this the concept of intention is enough to make your head spin like a lazy Susan, then take comfort in the fact that one branch of philosophy has no truck with any of these nuanced distinctions between acts and omissions, positive and negative duties, intended and merely foreseen effects. It takes its inspiration from a figure whose skeleton, bulked up with hay and straw and cotton and lavender (to keep the moths away) and dressed in a jacket and white ruched shirt, sits in a glass-fronted case off Gower Street in the heart of London. A walking stick, which was given a pet name, Dapple, rests in the case too. If the body were to spring to life, it could provide an instant response to the Fat Man puzzle. There would be no agonizing, no grappling with conscience. For the founder of utilitarianism, the appropriate action would be self-evident.

Morals by Numbers

It is the greatest good to the greatest number of people which is the measure of right and wrong.

—*Jeremy Bentham*

He was not a great philosopher, but he was a great reformer in philosophy.

—*John Stuart Mill on Bentham*

JEREMY BENTHAM (1748–1832) requested in his will that his cadaver be dissected for scientific research. He was friendly with many of the founders of University College, part of London University, where his Auto-Icon, as he called it, can still be seen. His skeleton was preserved. The stuffed body has a wax head with piercing blue eyes, crowned with a fetching wide-brimmed hat: the real head, which kept being pinched by student pranksters, is now under lock and key. One legend, that in the past the Auto-Icon was wheeled out for college governing meetings, where it was registered as "present but not voting," appears, alas, not to be true.

Bentham's strange afterlife befitted his eccentric life. His oddness was manifest in his idiosyncratic use of language. Rather than go for a walk before breakfast, he would announce his intention to have an antejentacular circumgyration. He was devoted to a senescent cat, whom he'd named the Reverend Dr. John Langborn.

In what is surely the most curious family linkage in the history of philosophy, Jeremy Bentham had a close friend James Mill, and acted as a guardian figure for Mill's son, who himself would become an acclaimed philosopher, John Stuart Mill. John Stuart Mill had a godson who was one of the most important philosophers of the twentieth century, Bertrand Russell. Mill had reservations about Bentham's philosophy, but nonetheless described him, in what was intended as a compliment, as the "chief subversive thinker of his age."[1] And Russell was a fan of Bentham's too. He gave him credit for many of the more enlightened reforms undertaken in Victorian England. "There can be no doubt that nine-tenths of the people living in England in the latter part of last [the nineteenth] century were happier than they would have been if he had never lived," Russell wrote, before adding a characteristic quip: "So shallow was his philosophy that he would have regarded this as a vindication of his activities. We, in our more enlightened age, can see that such a view is preposterous."[2]

Bentham maintained that what mattered about an action was how much pleasure it produced and how much pain was avoided. He enjoined us always to act so as to maximize pleasure and minimize pain. In his most influential book, *An Introduction to the Principles of Morals and Legislation*, he even devised an algorithm for how this could be calculated. He called it the "felicific calculus." How much pleasure would it give you to eat that piece of chocolate cake in front of you, how long would this pleasure last, would it be accompanied by any unpleasant feelings (make you feel a bit nauseous?). In fact, Bentham identified seven relevant components of a pleasurable action: the pleasure's intensity, duration, likelihood, propinquity (how quickly would the pleasure kick in), fecundity (would it produce similar sensations), purity (might it be followed by painful sensations), and extent (how many people would it affect). He regarded individuals as cargo containers of emotion: they should have a minimum of pain and be as jampacked as possible with pleasure.

The greatest happiness of the greatest number was the measure of all things. Wielding this calculus, the utilitarian could bludgeon out practical solutions to an array of local and national issues, be they political, social, administrative, or legal. There was a beguiling simplicity and elegance to his formula and utilitarianism quickly attracted numerous highly placed disciples. The Lord Chancellor, Henry Brougham, said, "the age of law reform and the age of Jeremy Bentham are one and the same."[3]

Bentham viewed utilitarianism as a type of science, undermining irrational traditions and the superstitions (including religious superstitions) of the past. The sovereign or legislator should have the role of the mechanic, twiddling and tinkering with the wires and handles, knobs and pipes of society to maximize happiness. Utilitarianism was progressive and forward looking with an egalitarian appeal: the pleasure of one person was to count no more and no less than that of another. The way to assess a law or government bill was to weigh its respective benefits and costs and compare them against competing proposals. It's been said that "he dreamt of doing for morals and legislation what Newton and Leibniz had done for natural science and mathematics."[4]

It would be impossible to fault Bentham on his intellectual honesty or his consistency, admirable qualities that led him to make some proposals quite shocking for the age. Since what mattered was feeling, pleasure and pain, we should care about animal as well as human suffering. "The question is not, Can they reason? nor, Can they talk? but, Can they suffer?"[5] If sex brought pleasure, then it didn't matter whether it was between a man and a woman, a man and a man, or a man and a beast (Bentham, the fanatical codifier, spelled out numerous other permutations too) and the laws should be liberalized to reflect this. He made scores of other practical suggestions about how laws could be reformed and government improved—some big, some small, and all driven by the imperative of maximizing happiness. For example, he thought it would be a good idea to have a national register for births and deaths: at the time, none existed.

The point of philosophy was to change the world, and Bentham was keen to spread the utilitarian gospel far and wide. He did, however, face a self-inflicted obstacle: his prose. He wrote prolifically, and coined dozens of wonderful, valuable neologisms (such as "international," "codification," "maximize," and "minimize"), but his most ardent admirers would not inflate their reverence by describing his style as lucid or sparkling. "Tortuous" is a more commonly attributed adjective. It grew worse as he grew older. A contemporary review of Bentham's book, *Rationale of Judicial Evidence*, complained that "Even the cabinets of diplomacy can scarcely ever have witnessed so successful an employment of words for the concealment of thoughts, as is here exhibited."[6]

In many ways utilitarianism was a uniquely British creed, at least in its origins. Britain was rapidly becoming more middle class, more materialistic, more subversive, less hidebound by tradition. Bentham accelerated these developments. But in the rest of Europe Bentham was chiefly known through translations of his Genevan editor and proselytizer, Étienne Dumont, who did Bentham the inestimable service of turning his language not only from English into French, but from convoluted and stodgy to fluent and accessible.

Bentham, meanwhile, ran a sleek PR campaign of his own, corresponding with scores of statesmen: his influence would be felt from across Europe to North and South America. A historian has noted that "Members of the Colombian Congress in the mid-1820s were quoting Bentham at each other much as eighteenth-century Englishmen had quoted classical authors in the House of Commons."[7] Bentham had a particular affection for, and interest in, the United States, and the feeling was mutual. He exchanged letters with President Andrew Jackson, confiding that in his old age he felt "more of a United States man than an Englishman,"[8] and when John Quincy Adams, the future president, was in London, he and Bentham would take strolls together in the park.

Not that Bentham was a supporter of the American system of government. *The Declaration of Independence* was slated as a "hodgepodge of confusion and uncertainty,"[9] *The Declaration of the Rights of Man* was "a perpetual vein of nonsense."[10] Bentham had been trained as a lawyer, and throughout his life, nothing would enrage him more than examples of what he regarded as legal iniquity, inconsistency, or incoherence. He regarded "rights" as nonsense. Crucially, he flat-out rejected the idea of "natural rights"—universal rights that all people have at all times independent of any particular laws—as "Nonsense on stilts."[11] Appeals to the fat man's rights would have been given short shrift by Jeremy Bentham.

Numbers mattered to Bentham. Other things being equal, it was always better to save more than fewer lives. It was the reason he was such a staunch opponent of war. He thought in most wars that many are made "to murder one another for the gratification of the avarice or pride of the few."[12] It was almost inconceivable that the expense of war could be justified by any gains. To the argument that Britain had become prosperous by victory in the Seven Years War (1756–63) he replied, "True enough it is that a man who has had a leg cut off, and the stump healed, may hop the faster than a man who lies in bed with both legs broken can walk. And thus you may prove that Britain was put into a better case by that glorious war, than if there had been no war, because France was put into a still worse."[13]

Bentham recognized that commonsense morality held there to be a distinction between "intending" and "foreseeing," or as he put it, between "direct intention" and "oblique intention." But he rejected any intrinsic moral difference between these two. So Bentham would not have thought too long and hard about the trolley problem. Assuming all lives are of equal value, killing one person, whether intentionally or not, is preferable to allowing five to die. Only the numbers matter. It is irrelevant whether the deaths are intended and irrelevant too whether they are brought about by killing people or by letting them die. We must ignore our moral intuitions: no valid ethical distinction can be drawn between Spur and Fat Man. The fat man should be pushed.

Beyond Pleasure

Two centuries after his death, Bentham's voluminous writings are still being edited and published, and there's a resurgence in Bentham scholarship. But his achievements remain underrated. His outlook is regarded as almost embarrassingly crude, the felicific calculus foolish, the reduction of life's value to "pleasure," shallow. The fact that he delivers such an instant and unequivocal answer to the problem of the fat man constitutes, in the minds of most philosophers, a fatal flaw rather than an asset.

But Bentham was the founder of a school of thought that, though not exactly *à la mode*, nonetheless has powerful adherents to this day. John Stuart Mill, was a utilitarian and Bertrand Russell had utilitarian instincts. Another giant, the nineteenth-century Cambridge philosopher, Henry Sidgwick, wrote within the utilitarian tradition. In the twentieth century, utilitarianism once again had a brief spell of dominance, the pivotal figure in its revival being the Oxford professor, Richard Hare. And today, important philosophers such as Derek Parfit and Peter Singer operate unashamedly in Bentham's long shadow.

There has been significant fine-tuning of utilitarianism since Bentham, of course, and some of these refinements add levels of subtlety to how a utilitarian should determine the fate of the fat man. Indeed, most students today are exposed to utilitarian thought not via Bentham, but through the writings of the son of his friend, James Mill.

Mill's Pill

Bentham had been a child prodigy. He was reading at three, was taught Latin and Greek from the age of four, and entered Oxford University at twelve. But compared to John Stuart Mill that made him something of a late developer.

J. S. Mill's father, James, was an austere, unemotional, and dominating man. Raised in Scotland, he became acquainted with Bentham only after moving to London. Mill Sr. had a thought experiment of his own. He believed that the mind was born a blank sheet. The question was, what could one imprint on this *tabula rasa*? What would happen if you subjected a child to the most rigorous form of home education—covering both the sciences and the humanities? What kind of a being could you create? What brilliance, what talent, what skills could be cultivated?

The thought experiment of James Mill differed from those in trolleyology in that it could be investigated in the real world. In what today's social service departments would no doubt regard as a form of child abuse, Mill set about feeding his boy with high-protein knowledge. John Stuart Mill was learning Greek and arithmetic at three years old.[14] The toddler was spared Latin, which was deferred until age eight. By fourteen, John had carried out intensive studies of logic and mathematics. He also made his way through lengthy reading lists in other disciplines like history and economic theory.

All this information was effectively crammed into John's mind, but was not conducive to his mental health: at age twenty, he suffered a breakdown. The emphasis he would later put on liberty and autonomy was perhaps a resentful reaction to his guinea-pig childhood. Nonetheless, at least in theoretical terms, the driving principle of his philosophy was not liberty but utilitarianism (a torrent of academic ink has flowed on the link between these two). Mill said of his guardian that his purpose was "to carry the warfare against absurdity into things practical,"[15] a principle that Mill could equally have applied to himself. When he read a translation of Bentham's work (in French) and came across the principle of utility, he said: "It gave unity to my conception of things. I now had opinions: a creed, a doctrine, a philosophy; in one among the best senses of the word, a religion: the inculcation and diffusion of which could be made the principal outward purpose of a life."[16]

Some geniuses exhibit their gifts in one narrow sphere: Mill's genius was the sort that revealed itself through many. He was a logician and economist and the most influential English-speaking moral philosopher and political theorist of the nineteenth century. He also found time to be an administrator, essayist, and polemicist, effective advocate of women's rights, and a member of parliament.

Mill remained indebted to Bentham all his life, and like Bentham was a consequentialist—believing that what mattered about an action were its consequences. But he was far from being an uncritical follower of Bentham's theory. An essay Mill wrote about Bentham had inflicted lasting damage on Bentham's intellectual legacy and reputation. For Bentham, all pleasures and pains were to be weighed on the same scale. Describing a child's game he claimed that, "prejudice apart, the game of pushpin is of equal value with the arts and sciences of music and poetry."[17] If pushpin gave more pleasure than poetry, it ought to be considered more valuable.

Mill had received too elite an education to stomach that. What's more, after his nervous collapse, he began to read poetry prodigiously, an art form which Bentham had splendidly dismissed as lines that fall short of the margin. For Mill, some forms of happiness were of a higher quality than others. "[i]t is better to be a human being dissatisfied than a pig satisfied; better to be Socrates dissatisfied than a fool satisfied."[18] One could identify the higher pleasure, Mill argued, by seeing which was preferred by a person exposed to both. He had a touchingly naive expectation that the majority of those who had experiences of both pushpin and poetry would choose the latter. He now put more emphasis on imagination and emotion and, reflecting on his early life, wrote: "I conceive that the description so often given of a Benthamite, as a mere reasoning machine was, during two or three years of my life not altogether untrue of me."[19]

But, in addition to drawing a distinction between types of pleasure, Mill proposed another adjustment to Benthamism, more pertinent to the problem of the fat man. It would be disastrous if, each time we had to act, we had to reflect on the consequences of our action. For one thing, this would take far too much time; for another, it might generate public unease. Far better to have a set of rules to guide us.[20]

Thus, it may be that to save five lives a judge needs to frame an innocent man, but society would operate more smoothly if individual judges were not tempted to pervert justice in this way. "Do not convict the innocent" would seem a sensible rule for judges to follow if we want to maximize well-being or happiness overall. If we believed that judges were willing to disregard the little matter of innocence or guilt for what they believed to be a higher value, our faith in the entire legal structure would be fatally undermined. And to feel secure we require the institutions of state to operate consistently, without making exceptions on grounds of expediency. We do not want judges even to consider the option of framing an innocent man, for mere reflection about such an option would contribute to an erosion of confidence in the system of justice.

Other utilitarian philosophers have developed this thought further. What should we do in the notorious ticking-bomb scenario discussed earlier? Imagine that we can extract information to defuse a bomb that threatens thousands of lives only by torturing a person who has this information. Henry Sidgwick (1838–1900) described what he called "esoteric morality"[21] and which the British twentieth-century philosopher Bernard Williams derided as "Government House utilitarianism."[22] Ostensibly, we want to uphold a rule like "do not torture" since to permit any exceptions could lead to terrible abuses. But in practice, it might be right, in very unusual circumstances, to torture someone, especially if the violation of the torture rule could be kept secret. It might also be the case—and this sounds terribly Machiavellian—that only an elite can be trusted to act in every decision on utilitarian principles, while the broad "vulgar" mass should be indoctrinated with general maxims, since they can't be expected to handle "the inevitable indefiniteness and complexity" of utilitarian calculations.[23]

> Thus, on Utilitarian principles, it may be right to do and privately recommend, under certain circumstances, what it would not be right to advocate openly; it may be right to teach openly to one set of persons what it would be wrong to teach to others; it may be conceivably right to do, if it can be done with comparative secrecy, what it would be wrong to do in the face of the world.[24]

In the twentieth century, Philippa Foot's contemporary, Richard Hare, was another promoter of two-tiered utilitarianism.[25] Life is complicated and time is short, so we would do well to operate with a series of rough-and-ready rules that on balance will produce the best overall result. One can see how it's sensible to have a rule about not killing bystanders, be they fat men on footpaths or healthy visitors to medical centers. Even if it were the case that doctors could murder a man with a rare blood type to save the lives of five dying patients, this would be more than offset, in utilitarian terms, by the panic and anxiety such a practice would provoke. It would be unsettling to have to worry that any time you visited a sick relative in hospital, it might be you who ended up under the scalpel with surgeons cutting out your organs. So, we should adhere to the rough-and-ready rules. Every now and again our rules will come into conflict: we may be able to follow one rule, but only at the cost of violating another. "Tell the truth" and "do not harm a person's feelings" might conflict if someone asks you whether you like their haircut. When rules conflict, says Hare, you should appeal to your internal utilitarian referee—and judge, by a utilitarian standard, which rule you should ditch on this occasion.

A Place for Qualms

A utilitarian trolleyologist is an oxymoron. The raison d'être of this philosophical sub-genre, trolleyology, is to identify differences between cases in which either one or five people die. But the utilitarian rejects the notion that there are intrinsic differences in these cases: the utilitarian doesn't take seriously the difference between intending and foreseeing, acting or omitting, doing or allowing, between negative and positive duties. True, the utilitarian has an elegant explanation as to why the idea of killing the fat man, or the healthy hospital visitor, makes people feel queasy, and indeed why this queasiness is to be encouraged, as conducive in the long run to the general good. But thought experiments being thought experiments, utilitarians must ultimately embrace the logic of their position: scenarios can be reworked so that the utilitarian can no longer appeal to rules.[26]

Thus, imagine that a utilitarian professor of philosophy were standing next to the fat man and knew that the fat man's death could be passed off as an accidental fall. No one would ever find out the truth. There would be no threat to social cohesion. Imagine too that the professor, being a committed and clear-eyed utilitarian, could correctly predict that he or she would feel no subsequent qualms about killing the fat man. In those circumstances, the professor would have to reach the conclusion that killing the fat man was the right thing to do.

Those who would still balk in such circumstances at the killing of the fat man are likely to agree with Bernard Williams, the British philosopher, that utilitarianism is fundamentally flawed. Back in the 1970s, Williams offered two thought experiments of his own designed to show that utilitarianism failed to capture various essential dimensions of our moral life.

The first case involved George and the second, Jim. George is a qualified chemist but finding it difficult to get work, and has a wife and small children to support. He is told by a colleague about a decently paid post in a laboratory that's researching chemical and biological warfare. George opposes such research and so says he couldn't accept a job in such a place. His colleague points out that if George doesn't take the job, it will go to a contemporary of George's who would pursue the research with far greater zeal. What should George do?

Now take Jim's predicament. Jim arrives in a central square in a small South American town. Tied up against the wall are a row of twenty terrified Indians in front of several armed men. The captain of the armed men arrives and begins to chat with Jim. He explains that he's selected these twenty people at random after some acts of protest against the government: he's going to kill them as a deterrent to future protest. However, since Jim is an honored visitor from another land, he will offer him the privilege of killing one of the Indians himself. If Jim accepts, the other Indians will be freed. If he doesn't, all twenty will be killed. What should Jim do?[27]

In the George scenario, Williams was making the point that utilitarianism can't account for integrity. From a utilitarian perspective, everything points toward George taking the job.

It'll bring in a much-needed income and actually hold back, rather than accelerate, research into biological and chemical warfare. But it would be "absurd," says Williams, to expect of George that simply because of the utilitarian calculus he should put aside his most deeply held convictions.

Jim's quandary has a closer parallel to the Fat Man case. Williams thought that Jim should, on balance, kill the Indian. But the problem with utilitarianism was how it assessed this situation, how it weighed and balanced reasons for action. For the utilitarian it is obvious that this is what Jim should do: it's one life against twenty. But that misses the fact, said Williams, that if Jim picks up the gun, it will be Jim who does the killing. The utilitarian, in the philosopher's jargon, takes no account of "agency." All the utilitarian cares about is *what* produces the best result, not *who* produces this result or how this result is brought about. Whether it is caused by Jim acting, or failing to act, is irrelevant. We are as responsible for what we fail to do, as for what we actually do. But that's not how we ordinarily view matters: if Jim can't bring himself to shoot the Indian we'd hold the Captain, not Jim, responsible for the deaths of the twenty. Utilitarians make the mistake, in Williams's view, of believing they can judge actions from the "point of view of the universe."[28]

But assessing outcomes from this bird's-eye perspective is precisely what hard-headed utilitarians advocate that we do. Peter Singer is the best known of a number of contemporary utilitarian thinkers. He thinks the right thing to do is to push the fat man and that there is no relevant distinction between doing so, and turning the trolley in Spur.

To most philosophers, that conclusion is a *reductio ad absurdum* of the utilitarian approach. It seems to them wildly counterintuitive: which raises two issues. Why should we take our instinctive feelings and reactions seriously on these matters? And do philosophers have any special authority over—any unique insight into—what's right and what's wrong?

To answer these questions, the walls between philosophy and other disciplines have had to be cut and planed if not exactly torn down.

PART 2

Experiments and the Trolley

CHAPTER 9

Out of the Armchair

Man will become better when
you show him what he is like.

—*Anton Chekhov*

A philosophical problem is not an empirical problem.

—*Judith Jarvis Thompson*

THE TRADITIONAL CARICATURE of the fusty philosopher seats
him in a very specific item of furniture. His profound thoughts
emerge from a sedentary position, but he is not on a stool,
bench, rocking chair, sofa, chaise-lounge or—God forbid—
bean-bag or deck chair (although, as it happens, Wittgenstein
inflicted deck chairs on his students who came to his spartan
Cambridge room). No, the philosopher sits in an armchair: it's
no doubt comfortably deep, and a little frayed at the edges, and
there's room on the armrest to balance a book and a smudgy
glass of sherry.

It's this image that explains the icon of a new movement.
This movement has a label that could have been dreamed up
by a public relations firm—x-phi—standing for "experimental
philosophy," philosophy with an empirical edge. In recent
years, blogs, periodicals, and books have been devoted to x-phi,

and research grants have been lavishly bestowed on its exponents. The icon of the x-phi movement is a burning armchair.

Critics complain that the experiments carried out under the x-phi banner lack scientific rigor and should not be categorized as philosophy. "The worry about experimental philosophy is that it's like Christian Science—it isn't either," is how one detractor puts it.[1] We'll return to such worries later. Nonetheless, insofar as a philosophical movement can be fashionable, x-phi is currently very much all the rage.

At least since the work in the late nineteenth and early twentieth centuries of the German logician, Gottlob Frege, the portrayal of the armchair philosopher has had some basis in reality. Frege regarded philosophy as a discipline requiring just the tools of logic and conceptual analysis. In that sense, it could be practiced without rising from the upholstery and it was unlike chemistry, which had Bunsen burners, history, which fed on archives, or sociology, which drew on surveys.

Philosophy was not always like this. Philosophy has become a separate discipline only relatively recently, and philosophers have historically made use of findings from the empirical sciences. Some philosophers even performed their own experiments—Aristotle, a pioneer in taxonomy, dissected all manner of creatures, from crustaceans to cuttlefish.[2] The x-phi movement claims to be a return to an earlier time, when philosophy had a broader self-conception, and was not separated from other disciplines. As one of the leaders of the x-phi movement expresses it, experimental philosophy is "more a retro movement, an attempt to go back to what philosophy was traditionally about."[3]

While x-phi has drawn extensively on the work of social psychology, until recently much of it has involved a different methodology—a deconstruction of everyday intuitions through surveys. Faced with a real or imaginary set of circumstances, philosophers are not shy to proclaim that their reaction must be the universal reaction of all right-minded people everywhere. "We can all agree that . . . ," they might say. A typical example is given by Judith Jarvis Thomson. Imagine five people are at risk in a hospital, not from their ailments but from the ceiling of their room, which is about to fall on them. We can prevent this potential calamity by pumping on a ceiling-support mechanism, but doing so will inevitably release lethal fumes into the room of a sixth person. Here, she writes, "*it is plain* we may not proceed."[4] But x-phi has begun to undermine that sort of assured presumption. Is it really the case that the intuitions in the Oxford colleges of Somerville and St. Anne's are shared by the inhabitants of Nashville and Saint Petersburg?

There are many areas of philosophy where the cross-cultural sociology of intuitions is injecting new energy into age-old questions, and not merely in ethics. Take the relationship between knowledge and belief: when can I be said to *know* something, when to merely *believe* it. Once, the standard answer was that I know it when I have justified true belief, and I have a justified true belief when the following three conditions are satisfied: (a) I believe it, (b) it is true, and (c) I have good reason for believing it to be true. Here's an example. Do I know that there's a man tied to the track ahead of me? Well, if there *is* a man tied to the track, and I look and see a man tied to the track, then surely I can be said to *know* there's a man tied to the track.

But in 1963 an American philosopher, Edmund L. Gettier III, then at Wayne State University in Detroit, imagined some problematic cases. Gettier had not published before and was under intense pressure from the university bureaucrats to produce some scholarly work. He reluctantly wrote a three-page paper, *Is Justified True Belief Knowledge?* He himself was lukewarm about it. "Up to the last moment of decision, I would never have dreamed of submitting a philosophy paper that consisted of nothing but a counterexample." And he has not published a word since, because "I have nothing more to say."[5] But his short paper has become among the most influential in contemporary philosophy.

Here is a Gettier-type scenario. Suppose, in the example above, what I see on the track is actually a fallen tree trunk, which bears a close resemblance to a man and from a distance I mistake it for such. And suppose that, by pure coincidence, nestling just behind the tree trunk a man lies prostrate, tied to the track. I have fulfilled all three conditions. I believe there's a man tied to the track, it is true that there's a man tied to the track, and I have good reason for believing that there's a man tied to the track (since I see a human-like object on the line). But can I be said to *know* that there's a man tied to the track or, as Gettier claimed, that I merely *believe* it?

Philosophers in the West have assumed that Gettier was right about such cases. I can only be said to *believe* that there's a man on the track, but it would be wrong to say I *know* it. Recently the x-phi crew has rolled up, armed with their pencils and clipboards. Instead of taking Gettier's intuition for granted, they posed the question to ordinary people, both in the East and the West—with unexpected results. It turns out that, while respondents in the West concurred with Gettier (that I only *believed* there was a man on the track), the majority of East Asian participants said that I *knew* there was a man on the track.[6]

Equally fascinating results were uncovered when people were questioned about other perennial philosophical problems, such as free will. Assuming the universe to be entirely deterministic, entirely governed by causal laws (a contentious premise), can a person be said to have free will, and is free will compatible with moral responsibility? Should I be praised or blamed if my actions were somehow the inevitable product of a causal chain?

Here it turns out that the more nitty-gritty details subjects were given about a situation, the more likely they were to be "compatibilists," to hold that even though a man or woman was caused to act, he or she could still be held to act freely and to be morally responsible. By contrast, the more abstract the example, the less likely subjects were to use concepts like "praise" and "blame." Thus, offered a richly textured story about a deterministic universe in which there was an embittered forty-five-year-old woman named Mary, who worked as a bank teller and was desperate for promotion, but who had a rival for the job, a genial, somewhat overweight thirty-five-year-old man named Mike, who had asthma and happened to pause for breath while on a walk, and was leaning over a railway footbridge when Mary chanced upon him, giving him a sharp shove in the back . . . etc., subjects would be far more likely to hold Mary morally responsible for the killing than if the scenario were presented shorn of all its evocative details, and all that was revealed was that in this deterministic universe a person was pushed to his death.[7]

Almost every philosophical question of interest rests ultimately on intuitions of one kind or another. For a further example there's the notorious problem of reference. When we use the term, "Philippa Foot," to what, or to whom, do we refer? One answer is that we refer to the person who fits a certain description, such as "the woman who devised the trolley problem." The American philosopher and logician Saul Kripke thought that this account was wrong; he proposed a variation of the following thought experiment to show why. Suppose another philosopher, call her Penelope Hand, conceived the trolley problem, and just before she died mentioned it to Philippa Foot, who then passed it off as her own. Surely, if we then used the name Philippa Foot, we wouldn't be referring to Penelope Hand, who fits the description of Philippa Foot better than Foot herself? And indeed, in surveys using a similar question, American philosophers concurred with Kripke's intuition: use of the term Philippa Foot would not, in their view, refer to Penelope Hand. But when this experiment was conducted in Hong Kong, the majority disagreed: for them, anybody who used the name Philippa Foot would actually be referring to Penelope Hand.

You Tell Me

Trolleyology has been embraced by the x-phi movement: there have been numerous studies to examine whether the intuitions of the philosopher are shared by the man on the Clapham omnibus. And there have been various experiments designed to test the influences on, and the stability of, our trolley intuitions.

Some of these experiments have been small in size. But the Internet has provided a flawed, though cheap and convenient way to collate opinion on a grand scale. One data-gathering tool has been managed by Harvard University. Since it was set up in 2004, more than 200,000 people have tested their moral intuitions in numerous scenarios at their Moral Sense Test: several tens of thousands of participants have been non-American. That's a decent sample by any statistical standards, though caution still has to be applied in interpreting the numbers, since those who take such a test may in some ways be unrepresentative of the general population—they have an eccentric interest in moral philosophy, for starters.

Another large survey has been conducted by BBC online: it included 65,000 participants. The findings on these various sites do not markedly differ. The BBC found that roughly four out of five agreed that the trolley should be diverted down the spur. Meanwhile, only one in four thought that the fat man should be heaved over the footbridge. Other studies have suggested that closer to 90 percent would divert in Spur, and up to 90 percent would not push the fat man.

Some gender differences have been found. In general, women emerge as harm-averse (less likely to push the fat man, or flip the switch in Spur), men as more utilitarian (more likely to push the fat man or flip the switch). And there is some other demographic variability. Hospital workers are more harm-averse than military workers (with many other professions falling in between). Religious people (those surveyed are mostly Christian) are more harm-averse than the non-religious. Conservatives are more harm-adverse than liberals. However, these differences are not dramatic. And on the whole there is no significant distinction between the rich and poor, the educated and uneducated, and those from the developed and the less developed worlds.

What is the philosophical value of appealing to such polls and surveys? None: it's a worthless exercise, say some, including the eminent Cambridge philosopher Hugh Mellor. "If this is philosophy then questionnaires asking people whether they think circles can be squares, is maths—which it isn't."[8]

But the gathering of survey information, the building of intuition data banks, has been used to cast doubt on whether our intuitions can ever be relied upon—and has raised the related question of whether the intuitions of experts are any more reliable than those of normal folk.

It Just *Feels* Wrong

The only really valuable thing is intuition.

—*Albert Einstein*

HERE'S A TROLLEY PROBLEM FROM FAMOUS Professor Robert Unger Joaching. It's pouring rain. A man is crossing the railway track, protecting himself with an umbrella. Given where he is, it would be prudent of him to pay more attention, but he's in a hurry and so doesn't spot a train racing toward him. It crashes into him at such speed and with such force that he is killed instantly and bits of his body go hurtling through the air. One large chunk hits a woman waiting on the platform, causing her severe injury. The question for the philosophy and law student is whether the woman should be able to make a financial claim against the dead man's estate.

But let's park this surreal trolley question for just a short while.

The Comfort Zone

Reading through the trolley literature is a little like watching a Rambo movie: you know it won't be long until the next slaying.

There are threats from every angle: from tractors and trains and collapsing bridges, from bombs and noxious gases. The cases have exotic names: there is the Loop Case of course, but also the Two Loop Case, the Extra Push Case, the Roller Skates Case, The Three Islands Case, the Tractor Case, and the Lazy Susan Case. But while trolleyology is a godsend to philosophy professors keen to entertain and enthuse students, does it have any relevance to the real world? How seriously should we take our intuitions about these outlandish fictions?

Exactly a century after John Stuart Mill finished making his amendments to *Utilitarianism*, another book was published that has received almost as much scholarly attention and that addressed the issue of how much weight we should give to our intuitions. A *Theory of Justice*, published in 1971, aimed to set out the rules by which a just society should be governed. It was written by a quiet, bookish Harvard professor, John Rawls, and although it has probably been read by only a tiny number of people outside academia, it has proved both radical and influential.

The book's most radical claim was that inequality was permissible only if it was to the benefit of the least advantaged. Its most important influence was felt not in university departments—although it rejuvenated political theory—but in the offices of state, among politicians and bureaucrats. It helped nudge decision makers away from a neutral utilitarian weighing up of policies by costs and benefits and toward a particular focus on the most deprived in society. Education, health, and transport policies were, of course, to be judged by whether they led to an overall improvement in standards, but also, and now especially, on what impact they had on the poorest and most marginal individuals and communities.

In A *Theory of Justice*, Rawls used a phrase relevant to the fate of the fat man: "Reflective Equilibrium." Theories about morality are not testable in the same way as theories about molecules. To test a theory about molecules we can use a microscope. To test a theory about morality we have to appeal to internal resources of the mind.

Crudely put, we are in reflective equilibrium when our general principles and our individual judgments about particular cases are in harmony. For example, we may start with a theory that we should never lie. But suppose lots of lives would be at risk on a particular occasion if we told the truth? Perhaps, then, we should amend our theory—water it down: "do not lie unless truth-telling would result in serious harm," or something like that.

On the other hand, we may wish to stick to the theory and ignore any conflicting intuitions. Mill had a principle of liberty: we ought to be free to do anything that causes no harm to others. What about private acts such as consensual, "safe," and nonpsychologically damaging sex between siblings? Firm believers in Mill's principle will probably have to overcome their instinctive opposition to such sibling sex. They may believe that their initial intuition about the repugnance of sibling sex should be disregarded, and that it shouldn't, on reflection, cause us to amend or weaken Mill's principle.

We are in a position of reflective equilibrium, said Rawls, when our set of beliefs about principles and our beliefs about individual cases have achieved a sort of coherence.

Reflective equilibrium is not the only model for how to handle intuitions, but it is the dominant one.[1] However, in recent times, the reliability of our intuitions has come under sustained assault from two directions. One prong of the attack is specific to trolley-like scenarios. Since they're so stylized, goes the charge, we cannot peel them off from the pages of a philosophy publication and transplant them onto a real case. The other prong is more general: that recent research in the social sciences has unearthed just how unstable and irrational our intuitions are across a whole spectrum of domains.

Tractors and Tumbles

To the specific allegation first. It is true that while the ingenuity of some of the trolley creations is admirable, they do lend themselves to satire. Take one of the splendid constructions from a doyenne of trolleyology, Frances Kamm, author of *Intricate Ethics*—the title considerably downplays the convolutions within.

As usual, a runaway trolley is heading toward five innocents. This is really not their day. Not only are they tied to the track, not only are they about to be flattened by the trolley, but there is another independent threat—rampaging in their direction is an out-of-control tractor. To redirect the trolley would be pointless if the five will in any case be hit by the tractor. But . . . .!!

There's a glimmer of hope for our ill-fated five. If you turn the trolley away from them, "it will gently hit and push (without hurting) one person into the path of the tractor. His being hit by the tractor stops the vehicle but also kills him."[2]

Now, this *is* clever. It has elements of Spur and elements of Fat Man. Turning the trolley away from the five looks permissible, even though one man would die—this parallels Spur. However, there would be no point turning the trolley if this man's corpse did not double as a buffer to halt the tractor—for otherwise the five would still be doomed. This mirrors Fat Man.

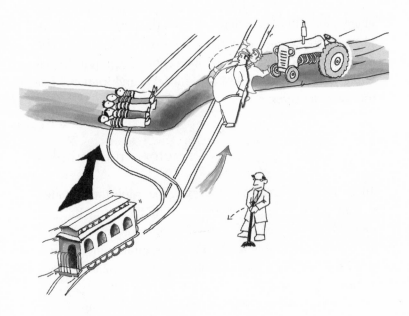

Figure 8. *Tractor Man.* The runaway trolley is heading toward five inno-cents. The trolley is not the only thing they're threatened by. They are also about to be flattened by another, independent, threat. Rampaging in their direction is an out-of-control tractor. To redirect the trolley would be pointless if the five were in any case to be hit by the tractor. But if you turn the trolley away from them, it will gently hit and push, without hurt-ing, another person into the path of the tractor. His being hit by the trac-tor would stop that vehicle but also kill him. Should you redirect the trolley?

But do you have a strong intuition about what should be done? No? Professor Kamm does. She is sure that it would be wrong to turn the trolley.

Or, instead, take Tumble Case.

This time you can't redirect the trolley but you can move the five. Unfortunately, the five will tumble down a mountain

Figure 9. *The Tumble Case.* The runaway trolley is heading toward five people. You cannot redirect the trolley, but you can move the five. But if you did that, the five would tumble down a mountain and, although they themselves would be unharmed, their body weight would kill an innocent person below. Should you move the five?

and their body weight will kill an innocent person below. Is it permissible to move the five? You're not sure? Professor Kamm says that it is. A few pages farther on there's the Trolley Tool Case. The trolley is heading toward a useful tool—one that could save many lives. You can redirect the trolley to kill one person. Should you do this? Confused? The answer (her answer) is that you should not.

But why should we take Kamm's word for it? Does a professor of philosophy, who has been wandering for decades down the highways and byways of trolleyology, have especially sensitive moral antennae? Well, perhaps. After all, we expect a wine connoisseur to be superior to ordinary topers in identifying and grading qualities in a wine. We expect something similar of an art buff who can look at a painting and be in a better position than the rest of us to assess its merits.[3]

Nonetheless, many of Kamm's tortuous cases even divide trolleyologists—so an appeal to expertise gets us only so far. That's not true of Spur and Fat Man, of course, where intuitions are more robust among both philosophers and lay people alike. But the indictment against trolleyology is that all its puzzles are improbable and, therefore, all of them are useless. According to Mary Midgely, even her old friend Philippa Foot would have been dismayed by the burgeoning sub-genre that she spawned: "this trolley-problem industry is just one more depressing example of academic philosophers' obsession with concentrating on selected, artificial examples so as to dodge the stress of looking at real issues."[4]

In the real world, we don't have T-junction ethics. In the real world we are not constrained by having just two options, X and Y: we have a multitude of options, and our choices are entangled in complex duties and obligations and motives. In the real world, crucially, there would be no certainty. If I pushed the fat man I could be tried for murder. Perhaps I would be concerned about a CCTV camera capturing my every move. I couldn't be sure that I'd be physically strong enough to shove the fat man over the bridge (if I tried to push him would there not be a danger that he'd retaliate and throw me over instead?). I couldn't be sure that the fat man's bulk would stop the trolley. I couldn't be sure that without my intervention the trolley would trundle onward and flatten the five.

They might manage to cut their ropes and escape. The driver might regain control of the trolley. And could I not find another bulky object that would be just as effective as the fat man's body in stopping the trolley?

Trolleys in the Real World

Confronted with the charge of artificiality, the best strategy for trolleyology is to embrace it. The thought experiments are deliberately contrived, yet most of them are not so wildly out of the world as to be entirely unrecognizable from actual cases.

There's a joke that lampoons moral philosophy. Question. How many moral philosophers does it take to change a lightbulb? Answer. Eight. One to change it and seven to hold everything else equal. But it's precisely because the trolley scenarios are so carefully engineered that they are of use. Real life is full of white noise, ethical hiss. The complexity of real life makes it difficult to identify pertinent features of moral reasoning. Trolley cases are designed to extract principles and detect relevant distinctions. They can only do so by blotting out the distracting and distorting sound. A crude analogy can be drawn with the scientific method. In the laboratory, if you want to test for the effect of, say, light, you vary the light while maintaining all other factors constant. Similarly, if you want to determine whether a particular feature is relevant morally, you imagine two cases that are otherwise identical while playing around with this one variable.

But neither are the basic trolley cases so fantastical that they're entirely detached from reality. Earlier I played a little trick on you, dear reader: Professor R U Joaching, referred to at the beginning of this chapter, is imaginary. But his trolley case is not. This accident took place in Chicago. The appellate court that heard the case ruled in the woman's favor. The young man who died, Hiroyuki Johu, was held responsible for her injuries: according to the court he should have foreseen that if hit by a train his body would be flung toward the platform and could hurt waiting passengers.

Of course, such cases are themselves outlandish. The point is, however, that they're not beyond the bounds of the possible. Recently there was another American case that could have been devised by a lecturer of Philosophy 101. It involved Dr. Hootan Roozrokh, declared innocent in a 2009 court judgment in California. What made his case philosophically interesting was the nature of the charges against him.

They concerned a sick man called Ruben Navarro. Navarro was from a working-class Latino background. He was twenty-five years old—about to be twenty-six. Fifteen years earlier his mother Rosa noticed that his balance had begun to deteriorate: when he played with other kids he fell over more frequently than they did. It was like watching Bambi on ice, she said. He was diagnosed with adrenal leukodystrophy—a progressive genetic disability, rare, but made famous by the Hollywood movie, *Lorenzo's Oil*. When Rosa herself became disabled, Ruben was put into care. His condition rapidly deteriorated. In January 2006, he was rushed to the Sierra Vista Regional Medical Center after being discovered unconscious, and in cardiac and respiratory arrest. Brain damage had been caused by lack of oxygen. The hospital said he would never recover. Rosa was asked and agreed to allow Ruben's organs to be used after death.

That was when a young doctor, Hootan Roozrokh, made an appearance. Roozrokh had flown in on behalf of the California

Transplant Donor Network, a laudable organization whose stated mission is to save and improve lives through organ and tissue donation for transplantation. Roozrokh was there to collect Ruben's organs after Ruben was declared dead, but when Ruben was removed from the respirator the plans went awry. Ruben's body stubbornly hung on to life. Organs have to be removed within 30 to 60 minutes of the respirator being turned off: beyond that time, they are not fresh enough to survive a transplant operation. But Ruben's heart was only slowly failing and his brain was continuing to function.

The allegation against Dr. Roozrokh was that he had ordered a nurse to administer unusually high doses of two drugs, morphine and Ativan, to Ruben, with the aim of hastening death. As it happened, it took Ruben several hours more to die, by which time his organs were of no use for transplantation. In finding Dr. Roozrokh not guilty, the court accepted his testimony that he had no intention of speeding up death: he simply wanted to ensure the patient would not suffer after life support was withdrawn.

Nonetheless, the charges bore a resemblance to the fictional hospital visitor who could be killed for his organs, a case cited by Judith Jarvis Thomson, Philippa Foot, and others. And although it was unusual, it raised questions similar to those raised in the trolley literature. Had Ruben been killed quickly, several lives could have been saved. The latest figures suggest that in the United States alone, eighteen people die every day awaiting organ transplants—a fatality figure far higher than the U.S. military death toll in Iraq or Afghanistan. Currently more than 100,000 people are on national waiting lists in the United States for heart, lung, liver, kidney, pancreas, or intestine organ transplants.

But even if the trolleyologist rebuts the charge of artificiality, there's a more fundamental objection still.

• • •

It's not just trolley intuitions that are suspect: it's all intuitions.

That is the obvious conclusion to draw from the research not of a philosopher, but of a psychologist—Daniel Kahneman. Kahneman won the Nobel Prize in economics and, with his colleague Amos Tversky, essentially invented the now thriving sub-discipline of behavioral economics—the investigation of how people make economic decisions in practice.

Pre-Tversky/Kahneman, economists of all persuasions were in the grip of an image of producers and consumers as rational economic actors, who made coherent, logical choices based on their particular preferences. Kahneman gave that picture a battering. He and his colleagues carried out numerous experiments that revealed Homo sapiens to be illogical, confused, and sometimes foolish creatures, driven by impulses of which they were often ignorant.

A famous test involved a scenario about a deadly virus. The U.S. authorities are preparing for an outbreak of a disease. Kahneman called it an "Asian disease"—perhaps this was designed to sound particularly threatening. In any case, if nothing is done about the disease, it will kill six hundred people. There are two alternative courses of action.

- YOU CAN ADOPT PROGRAM A. If you do so, two hundred lives will be saved.

- YOU CAN ADOPT PROGRAM B. If you do so, there is a one-third probability that six hundred people will be saved and a two-thirds probability that no people will be saved.

What do you do? Now imagine that the Asian disease will kill six hundred people, but this time you have the following options.

- YOU CAN ADOPT PROGRAM C. If you do so, four hundred people will die.

- YOU CAN ADOPT PROGRAM D. If you do so, there's a one-third probability that nobody will die and a two-thirds probability that six hundred people will die.

What do you do? In studies, most people thought A was preferable to B, but that D was preferable to C. And this is odd, since A, although expressed in different terms, is exactly the same outcome as C, while B is identical to D. Clearly how the alternatives were framed had an (irrational) impact on how subjects responded.

The same effect has been observed in trolleyology. Philosopher Peter Unger showed students a variation of the Fat Man (giving them the option to divert a large man on motorized roller skates into the path of a deadly trolley).[5] But some students were first exposed to various interim cases (thus, in one interim case students could stop the trolley by diverting another runaway trolley with two people into its path — killing the two). Students who had seen these interim cases were more likely to sanction the large man's killing when they were eventually confronted with it.

Doubts have also been raised about Judith Jarvis Thomson's Loop case. Thomson sets out Loop only after Spur. She insists that a few extra meters of track can make no moral difference — and this has struck many philosophers as a compelling claim. Thomson then reasoned that since it was permissible to turn the trolley in Spur, it was equally permissible to do so in Loop.

But a recent study demonstrated that if Loop is shown *prior* to Spur, subjects tend not to see such a close analogy between the two cases, and are more likely to believe that turning the trolley in Loop *is* wrong.[6]

Interestingly, too, showing Fat Man prior to Spur makes people far less likely to endorse turning the trolley in Spur. The ordering affects not just non-philosophers but those with PhDs in philosophy too. And we can play around with responses to moral dilemmas in other ways. Responses will vary according to whether questions are put in the third person—"Would it be wrong for *Philippa* to turn the trolley?"—or first—"Would it be wrong for *you* to turn the trolley?"

All of which leaves us with the problem of which intuitions to take seriously. How do we decide whether showing Spur first has sensitized and improved our intuitions about Spur, or coarsened and distorted them? If we want a good look at a stick, we know not to immerse it half in water: for that will make it seem bent even when it's not. If we want a good look at the colors in a painting, we need to observe the work of art in a room that's well lit. What equivalent account can be given of intuitions? How do we know that we're seeing a moral problem under ideal conditions—that we're seeing them, as it were, well lit?

That's a puzzle for which philosophers have not yet provided a satisfactory answer. But playing around with the wording and the ordering does not eliminate the gap in response between Fat Man and Spur. The gap can be narrowed, but only to a degree. In whatever form the problem is presented, the majority still think it right to turn the train in Spur and wrong to kill the Fat Man. And that gap, with only minor variations, exists among all groups of people, in all cultures.

This has led to a new hypothesis. The trolley problems may illustrate that human morality is innate—and that, for example, the Doctrine of Double Effect, first expounded nearly a millennium ago by Saint Thomas Aquinas, is hardwired into us.

Dudley's Choice and the Moral Instinct

Among so many inhuman and bizarre cults, among this prodigious diversity of morals and characters, you will find everywhere the same ideas of justice and decency, everywhere the same notions of good and bad.

—Jean-Jacques Rousseau

IN TOKYO, BLOWING YOUR NOSE loudly in public is considered the height of vulgarity. From culture to culture, practices of burping, belching, farting, spitting, body-scratching, bottom-wiping, lip-smacking, bowing, shaking hands, holding hands, food chewing, soup slurping, nail-biting, tooth-picking, and kissing vary widely. In parts of France, a couple of friends might greet each other with two cheek pecks: in some suburbs of Paris, four has become the norm—four more than is perhaps advisable in Riyadh.

Etiquette and manners encompass innumerable aspects of life: table manners, body language, dress code, facial hair, tipping and haggling, styles of exchanging gifts, ways to address friends and strangers. Those applying for British citizenship are supposed to know that in the pub people take turns buying a round of drinks.

It's tricky to demarcate a firm boundary between etiquette and morality. For a westerner (at least for this westerner), watching men in parts of Asia (hardly ever women) shut one nostril while snorting mucus out of the other still elicits a degree of visceral disgust. But this feeling is compatible with holding the belief that there is no right way, no objectively correct means, of maintaining nasal hygiene. The notion of blowing your nose into a handkerchief and stuffing it in your pocket seems revolting to some people. Different cultures have different practices. But what practice counts as etiquette and what morality? A Londoner and a Parisian would regard the difference in how they greet members of the opposite sex—two kisses or three—as one of etiquette. A Saudi imam might believe public kissing is not merely revolting, but immoral.

Morality is taken more seriously than manners and is usually thought to imply a universal quality.[1] Those who oppose female circumcision, or female genital mutilation, as it's come to be called, hold that it's immoral wherever it takes place, even if the practice in some parts of the world is widespread. However, although, when we make a moral statement we intend its universal application, it appears self-evident that moral practices, like practices of etiquette, vary widely. Abortion carries less stigma in Denmark than in Malta; the average inhabitant of Texas is pro capital punishment, many more people from Maine oppose it; homosexuality is seen as perfectly legitimate by most people in San Francisco, yet an abomination by many in Kampala.

Perhaps all the stranger then, that some academics claim that humans have an innate, universal moral sense: and to bolster this claim, they cite evidence from trolleyology.

Born Moral

How is it that we recognize that the sentence "runaway trolleys that are stationary smell morbidly" is a grammatical sentence, though nonsense, but "stationary smell are runaway trolleys that morbid" is not?

Noam Chomsky made his academic reputation through his pioneering work in linguistics in the 1950s and '60s. He asserted that the language instinct was innate. "Colourless green ideas sleep furiously" is a grammatical sentence. It's a well-formed sentence in syntactical terms. "Furiously sleep ideas green colourless" is not. We have an instinctive grasp for what's grammatically permissible in language and what isn't.

What struck Chomsky was that normal children acquire language remarkably easily, following rules that they are often not explicitly taught. Not only do they rapidly learn to distinguish grammatical from nongrammatical sentences, but they soon grasp other vital skills of the language user, such as the ability to identify contradictions or ambiguities. From a finite set of words and phrases they are able to construct an infinite number of sentences. None of this would be possible, argued Chomsky, unless we were somehow programmed to speak a language.

This program, or recipe, must be of a very general kind. A baby born in Guangzhou will grow up to speak Cantonese, a baby born in Budapest will learn Hungarian, and a baby born in Glasgow will speak English (though in an accent impenetrable to some fellow citizens). On the face of it, Chinese, Hungarian, and English have little in common. Nonetheless, said Chomsky, all these languages must share some kind of common structure.

Once children can speak a language, they develop strong and reliable and rapid instincts for what is linguistically kosher and what isn't. Strangely, however, language users cannot always justify their intuitions. They seem to follow rules subconsciously. Take the following example: most native English speakers would not say, "The black, terrifying, large trolley was out of control." That sounds a bit wrong, linguistically off-key. They would be more likely to say, instead, "The terrifying, large, black trolley was out of control." But why is the latter word order the correct one? Most people would struggle to give an instant response. In fact, they'd probably struggle to give an accurate response even given time to reflect on the matter.[2] The rules we've somehow absorbed are Byzantine. In "Colourless green ideas sleep furiously," we must know that "adjective, adjective, noun, verb, adverb" is a pattern that works, whereas its opposite, "adverb, verb, noun, adjective, adjective" does not.

In the 1990s, one of Chomsky's graduate students at the Massachusetts Institute of Technology, John Mikhail, wondered whether the linguistic model could be transposed to morality—and set about testing parallels with examples from trolleyology.

If there was a strong parallel, then children might be expected to have the same intuitions about the trolley cases as adults. And this is exactly what Mikhail found. He follows the psychologist Jonathan Haidt in describing children as "intuitive lawyers," although for Mikhail, a legal scholar, this is a positive description, while for Haidt it is a term of gentle mockery.[3] Kids make startlingly sophisticated moral judgments that mirror not just adult morality, but complex legal systems. Three- and four-year-olds use the idea of intentionality to distinguish two acts that have the same consequences: the person who mistakenly bumps into a man, causing him to tumble over the footbridge, and the person who deliberately does so. The law, and ordinary morality, make the same distinction. Four- and five-year-olds recognize a far more complex distinction, again similar to a legal distinction—between a mistake of fact and a mistake of law. Thus, a trolley driver might run over a bundle, assuming it's just leaves, and not realizing it's a man. This might be a mistake of fact, and offered as an excuse. If there were a good reason for this mistake to have occurred, this reason would certainly be considered relevant in assessing the driver's guilt. But if the trolley driver explains that he was perfectly aware of the man on the track but mistakenly believed it was permissible to flatten people with vehicles, well that's an error of law, and hardly an excuse.

The moral hardwiring, so the thesis goes, operates at a very abstract level, just as language does. Our rules do not have specific content (like, "do not insult your mother-in-law"), and there will be some local variations in morality, just as there are among languages. A universal law in language might be that a grammatical sentence contains a subject, verb, and object—but the order in which these appear differs from language to language: German speakers put the verb at the end of a sentence. Likewise, there will be some differences in morality from culture to culture. One study, carried out in India, examined the role of social and cultural expectations in trolley judgments. When the agent was of the scholarly (Brahmin) caste, participants disapproved of him pushing someone to save five lives; they were much more likely to approve if the pusher came from the warrior (Kshatriya) caste. Nonetheless, the claim is that the deep abstract rules (like, "do not intentionally harm the innocent") are universal.

Working with Mikhail, Marc Hauser, a (then) Harvard researcher in the same field, found, in another parallel with language, that moral intuitions were almost instantaneous and predictable over any number of unique cases—cases subjects had not previously confronted. What's more, if people were quizzed about why they held the intuitions they did, they often found them difficult to explain or justify. They would say things like, "I have no idea why I've changed my mind," or "I don't understand why this case seems different from the earlier one." Or they might be self-deprecatory, and somewhat embarrassed: "I know I'm not being rational, but these cases seem to me to be unalike." When justifications did emerge, they could vary wildly. Hauser writes: "This incapacity to generate an appropriate explanation is not restricted to the young or uneducated, but rather includes educated adults, males and females, with or without a background in moral philosophy or religion."[4] There were appeals to God, to emotions, to hunches, to rules (don't kill!), to consequences (five saved better than one saved), and, Hauser reports, one blunt rationalization: "shit happens."

By tweaking variables from the original trolley case, Mikhail and his co-researchers were able to extract elements of what Mikhail believes may be our innate morality. Here are two of his examples. All his cases involve a train out of control and about to kill five people.

MARK AND INTENTIONAL HOMICIDE

There is a man on the side track. Mark can throw [a] switch, killing him; or he can refrain from doing this, letting the five men die. Mark then recognizes that the man on the side track is someone whom he hates with a passion. "I don't give a damn about saving those five men," Mark thinks to himself, "but this is my chance to kill that bastard." Is it morally permissible for Mark to throw the switch?

WALTER AND THE COLLAPSED BRIDGE

Walter is standing next to a switch, which he can throw, that will collapse a footbridge overlooking the tracks into the path of the train, thereby preventing it from killing the men. There is a man standing on the footbridge. Walter can throw the switch, killing him; or he can refrain from doing this, letting the five die. Is it morally permissible for Walter to throw the switch?[5]

When Mikhail put these cases to his subjects, a substantial majority found it unacceptable for Mark to throw the switch, but permissible for Walter. With a slight variation from the original Spur and Fat Man scenarios, Mikhail had turned the intuitions around. He elicited quite different intuitions by changing facts about people's intentions. And it's easy to imagine how modifying other factors might influence intuitions too. Suppose in Spur:

- THE FIVE PEOPLE on the track were suffering from some dreadful disease and were going to die soon anyway, while the person on the spur was a child. Or

- WE DISCOVERED that the one man on the spur had unjustly and against his will been tied onto the track by five fascist bullies who had later become trapped on the main line only after crossing the rails in pursuit of another hapless victim? Or

- THE FIVE WERE strangers, but the one was your daughter. Or

- THE MAN ON THE SPUR was Einstein (or Stalin!), while the other five were ordinary Joes and Joannas like you and me.

Most of the scenarios in the trolley literature tend to exclude personal information about the individuals whose lives are at risk—including any wrongs they may have committed or any specific rights and entitlements they can or cannot appeal to. They are not even supplied with a name, let alone more substantial biographical details. But a more sophisticated picture of our moral grammar could encompass many more variables and a rich account of how they interact.

A nineteenth-century story of a digested British cabin boy illuminates a particularly interesting nuance in our moral grammar, while an Italian polymath helps put this tale into context.

The Italian Job

Vilfredo Federico Damaso Pareto (1848–1923), economist, political theorist, and one of the founders of modern sociology, had his own connection with railways. After graduating top of his class from Turin, he took a job in the Rome Railway Company. Pareto had trained as an engineer and was fascinated by mechanisms and laws: he had, according to one writer, a "thirst for laws."[6]

From the railway, Pareto went on to a role in an iron and steel company, before settling down in the lush hills of Tuscany to pen polemical articles lambasting the incompetence of the government in the recently united Italy. In 1893, aged forty-five, Pareto was offered, and accepted, the chair of political economy in the Swiss city of Lausanne. And although many of his ideas had already been formulated, it was from this moment that he began to generate the body of work that makes him relevant for our story and for which he is now remembered.

Pareto's hero was the man who had discovered the laws of motion, Sir Isaac Newton. Pareto, not unlike Karl Marx before him, aimed to do for the social world what Newton had done for the physical: Pareto's instincts were those of a scientist and he imagined that the social world, though in a constant state of flux, was moving between different equilibrium points.

It is easier for acolytes to choose their heroes than for heroes to choose their acolytes. This unfortunate law of the social world has sullied Pareto's posthumous reputation. While Pareto admired Newton, Benito Mussolini admired Pareto. He is thought to have attended some of Pareto's lectures in Lausanne in 1904. Subsequently the sociologist was wooed by the fascist party, though he died in 1923, less than a year after Mussolini had taken power. The twentieth-century Anglo-Austrian philosopher, Karl Popper, excoriated Pareto as the theoretician of totalitarianism, though it was hardly Pareto's fault that the fascists found succor in his Pareto Principle—that 80 percent of effects come from 20 percent of causes. Pareto had observed that four-fifths of Italian land was owned by one-fifth of the Italian people; later research indicated that this 80/20 distribution pattern was true not just of Italy, and, moreover, that it was repeated in a number of areas in addition to property and wealth. The fascists drew what to them was a comforting implication— that this was some kind of iron law.

But Pareto is credited with another eponymous principle. In economics, a state of affairs is said to be Pareto efficient or Pareto optimal when there could be no reallocation of goods that would make one or more individuals better off without making anyone else worse off. For example, suppose an economic system results in person A getting two philosophy books and person B getting three oranges. If we could somehow alter production and distribution so that person A received an orange in addition to his two philosophy books, while person B continued to receive three oranges, the prior state would have been shown to be Pareto inefficient.

What does all this have to do with trolleyology? Well, take the unusual case of Captain Tom Dudley.

Cannibalism on the High Seas

On July 25, 1884, Captain Dudley, a short man with red hair, stabbed, killed, and later began to eat his cabin boy. Some months later, this devout Anglican would be charged with and then found guilty of willful murder. He was sentenced to be "hanged by the neck until you be dead." But the then Home Secretary, Sir William Harcourt, knew the public would never tolerate such a punishment—and along with his fellow defendant, Edwin Stephens, Tom Dudley had his sentence commuted to six months in jail.

It was an unusual case, and one still cited in the courts. Dudley had openly admitted to the killing, and was stunned as well as indignant that it should be considered a crime. He had just survived an horrific experience, and was now having to relive it. He must have felt a sense of vindication when the cabin boy's brother approached him in court and, far from haranguing him, made a very public show of courteously shaking his hand.

Standing in the dock, and speaking in a pronounced Essex accent, Tom Dudley recounted his story. Twenty days before the murder, he, Richard Parker (the cabin boy), and two other men, Stephens and Edmund Brooks, had been in the middle of the Atlantic en route from England to Australia. Their mission was to deliver a yacht, *The Mignonette*, to its new owners.

They were well over a thousand miles from land when a terrible storm erupted and their yacht rapidly began to sink. They clambered into a lifeboat. In the chaos, all they managed to salvage from *The Mignonette* were two tins of turnips. Three weeks on, they were close to starvation. At seventeen, Parker was the youngest as well as the weakest. There had been little rainfall, and they had all been drinking their own urine, which Parker had supplemented with seawater. He had now begun to drift in and out of consciousness. The others were in a terrible state too. Scorched in daylight, cold at night, their feet had swollen, their bodies had sores.

This is where some details of the story become hazy, but according to Tom Dudley, he proposed a radical solution: they should draw lots and then one of them should be sacrificed for food. Brooks objected. He thought it was better they all die together. Dudley said, "So let it be, but it is hard for four to die, when perhaps one might save the rest."[7]

A few hours later, Dudley spoke to Stephens, a conversation that Brooks would claim not to have heard. Dudley asked, "What is to be done?" and he gave his answer, "I believe the boy is dying. You have a wife and five children, and I have a wife and three children. Human flesh has been eaten before."[8]

That night Dudley and Stephens stabbed Parker in the jugular with a penknife. For four days Dudley and Stephens fed off Parker's carcass (and drank his blood). Brooks, despite his denunciation of the crime, joined in: indeed, he ate heartily, more than Stephens, who was desperately feeble. The author of a book on the episode, Brian Simpson, writes that "The grim thought must have occurred to Stephens that he, as the weakest, was likely to be next on the menu."[9]

Miraculously, still drifting hundreds of miles from land, they were spotted by a German boat returning from South America to Hamburg. The compassionate captain and his crew watered and fed them, and slowly they regained a little of their strength. When they eventually sailed into the Cornish port of Falmouth, they provided a full written explanation of what had happened—common practice when a ship was lost. Not imagining that any legal process would ensue, Dudley spared few details. The decision to prosecute them was not taken lightly. But the Home Secretary had a reasonable worry: "If these men are not tried for murder, we are giving carte blanche to every ship's captain, whenever he runs low on provisions, to eat his cabin boy."[10]

The Anonymous Ferry Killer

With Stephens, Dudley had murdered an innocent boy. In most normal circumstances murder is unconscionable. But although Dudley was tried and found guilty of the crime, this case tends to evoke mixed feelings. While some will think murder unacceptable whatever the circumstances, others will have considerable sympathy for Dudley's predicament. If asked why, they'll say something like "well, the cabin boy was going to die anyway, so what harm was done?"

Or, to put it in more formal if rather heartless terms, many, probably most, people seem to recognize a rationale, a moral rationale to moving from a Pareto inefficient to a Pareto efficient state of affairs. This seems to be part of our moral grammar. Before Dudley orchestrated the killing of the cabin boy, all four men were dying. The cabin boy would have died anyway: his death allowed others to survive.

Their lot was improved and no one was made worse off. So Dudley's actions seem at least excusable.

There are other equally dramatic examples with a parallel moral structure. Take, for example, the killing that occurred just off the coast of Belgium on the evening of March 6, 1987. The killer has not been publicly named: he later confessed to the act, but was never charged. The authorities must have judged that, in the circumstances, this was a justified killing, and not only should there be no trial, but the identity of the killer should remain secret.

However, we have some details of the deed. It was the night that the *Herald of Free Enterprise*, a car and passenger ferry, capsized. Almost two hundred people, passengers and crew, lost their lives. The ship had been in the Belgian port of Zeebrugge and was due to make the short crossing to Dover on Britain's southern coast. The cause of the accident was a catastrophic human error: a crew member on duty had fallen asleep and the bow doors hadn't been closed. Within ninety seconds of leaving the harbor, the ship began to list. Within another minute the ship was plunged into darkness. Most of those who died were trapped inside and suffered hypothermia.

A coroner's inquest took place in October 1987. Numerous witnesses were called to give evidence, but the most unexpected testimony came from an army corporal. He claimed that with dozens of other people he was at the bottom of a rope ladder, all of them in the icy water. However, the ladder, their route to safety, was blocked by a young man. He was paralyzed either with fear, or cold (or perhaps with both), and appeared unable to move up or down the ladder. With time running out, the corporal shouted for him to be pushed off. He was, and was never seen or heard from again. The way was open for others to clamber up the ladder and to safety.

Again, callous though it sounds, the man on the rope ladder was not made worse off by being pushed to his death: he was soon going to die in any case and by blocking the escape route he would cause the deaths of fellow passengers. The decision to prosecute neither the corporal nor the person who actually carried out the deed must have been underpinned by Pareto considerations. In accepting (if we do) that the corporal had not acted immorally, we are conceding that there are some occasions when killing someone intentionally is not wrong.

Maltese Dilemma

There have been parallel mountaineering cases where two men are connected by a rope, and to survive one needs to cut loose the other (essentially condemning this second person to their death).[11] And there are fictional cases, too. In the book, and movie, *Sophie's Choice*, Sophie was forced by a Nazi officer to choose life for one of her children and death for the other. If she refused to pick, both would be sent to the gas chamber. She chose her son—the daughter was led away, screaming.

Sometimes the state, in the form of the courts, has mandated a killing in a Pareto-esque scenario. In 2000, a Catholic woman, Rina Attard, from the Maltese island of Gozo, gave birth in Britain to conjoined twins—the courts called them

Mary and Jodie. Doctors said the twins would both die unless they underwent surgery; but even if this operation went ahead only one of the babies, Jodie, would survive. The parents, both committed Roman Catholics, refused to allow this operation. Their written evidence included this:

> We cannot begin to accept or to contemplate that one of our children should die to enable the other one to survive. That is not God's will. Everyone has the right to life, so why should we kill one of our daughters to enable the other one to survive?[12]

The doctors challenged their decision. The argument went all the way to the high court where, in reaching their decision, the judges referred to works of philosophy, drew trolley-type analogies, quoted Hobbes, and cited *Regina v. Dudley and Stephens* and the Zeebrugge disaster, to determine, for example, whether carrying out the operation would be an example of an intentional killing.

In the end the court ruled that the operation should go ahead. It took place on November 7, 2000. Mary died, as the doctors had foreseen. Jodie survived, as predicted.

The Nazi Thought Experiment

Most people will be influenced by Pareto-type reasoning, just one feature of what some people call our moral grammar. The data bank of global moral instincts collated at Harvard's Moral Sense Test is revealing an intricate lattice-like moral edifice. At Harvard, I watched a researcher question a subject on a harrowing dilemma with a parallel structure to the cases described. The subject was asked to imagine that she was among a group of people hiding from the Nazis: her child was whimpering. Unless she smothered the child, the entire group would be discovered and murdered. The MST has presented this and similar scenarios on the Internet: for example, one case imagines a lifeboat that will sink and all its occupants die unless one person is jettisoned, so lightening the load.

One unusual feature of these cases is that they have revealed a big gender gap. Roughly 50 percent believe that it is acceptable to throw someone overboard in the lifeboat case, or for the mother to kill her child, but many fewer women than men think this. Nonetheless, Marc Hauser states, "When it comes to our evolved moral faculty—our moral competence—it looks like we speak in one voice: the voice of our species."[13]

The moral taxonomer, John Mikhail, has deconstructed actions in terms of their means (throwing the switch in Spur), ends (preventing the five men from being killed), and side effects (killing the man on the main track). Battery—unwanted bodily contact when this entails harm—is usually impermissible. In Fat Man, the side effects include killing *with* battery, which is why the fat man's killing is so obviously (to most people at least) ruled out.

A successful capturing of the principles that govern our ethical responses to the world holds out the prospect that, in theory, computers could be programmed to react like humans. In other words, if we could reduce moral considerations to algorithms, robots could be built to behave as we would like humans to behave.

This would have radical implications, such as in warfare. The future of warfare is robotic warfare, in which machines will have growing "autonomy" to make decisions without direct human oversight.[14] It would be naive to believe that machine "agents," such as those in the novels of Isaac Asimov or in movies like *Blade Runner*, are any longer confined to the realm of fiction.

The Google Driverless Car is in an advanced stage of development. In cities around the world, driverless trains, already a feature at numerous airports, are now being introduced. In Copenhagen, for example, computers control almost everything centrally. One could imagine that a runaway driverless train may face the "choice" between killing five and killing one—and that it could be programmed to respond to pertinent characteristics of the situation.

Artificially intelligent machines—be they driverless trains or gun-wielding robots—might even "behave" better than humans. Under stressful conditions—under fire for example—humans might push the fat man, an action which on reflection they might regret. Machine "decisions" need not be impaired by any rush of adrenaline.

The only (!) thing the software engineers need to agree on is what the moral rules are . . .

PART 3

Mind and Brain and the Trolley

The Irrational Animal

I can calculate the motion of heavenly
bodies but not the madness of people.

—*Isaac Newton*

'Tis not contrary to reason to prefer the destruction
of the whole world to the scratching of my finger.

—*David Hume*

When a man has just been greatly honored and
has eaten a little he is at his most charitable.

—*Nietzsche*

WHEN IT COMES TO THE FAT MAN, the philosopher wants to know the answer to a moral question: *should* we push him to the great beyond? The philosopher is interested in normative (value) questions—such as, how *should* we lead our lives?

Can the scientist help? The scientist, here, is broadly defined to include the psychologist and the neuroscientist. Typically the scientist is interested in different, non-normative, questions. Why do we give the answers we give? How do we reach our judgments? What influences our behavior? The Scottish Enlightenment philosopher, David Hume (1711–

1776), insisted that there was a distinction between fact and value—so no description of how we *do* judge can determine how we *should* judge. After all, if it turned out that we humans were innately disposed to be racist (or at least to favor our in-group over some out-group), that wouldn't be evidence that racism was in any way acceptable. But a generation of scientists have begun to investigate the trolley problem—and some of them claim that certain empirical discoveries have normative implications.

Bread and Clutter

For those wishing to believe that humans are governed by the dream team of reason and benevolence, much of the work of social psychology is unsettling. The experiments conducted by the Yale psychologist Stanley Milgram in the 1960s demonstrated that many people are willing to put their consciences to one side, when told by an authority figure to perform a bad action—in this case to turn a dial to give other people an electric shock.[1] The prison experiments conducted by the Stanford psychologist, Philip Zimbardo, also showed how badly people can behave when given a (pseudo) legitimate power. In a role-play, some subjects were assigned the role of guard, others that of prisoner, and they were put in a mock dungeon. Many of the "guards" quickly began to exhibit sadistic tendencies toward the "prisoners."

In another oft-recited experiment, divinity students at the Princeton Theological Seminary were informed that they had to give a presentation on the parable of the Good Samaritan.[2] As they were dispatched off across the quad to deliver it, some of them were told that they were a few minutes late. Before they reached their next destination they encountered a man slumped in an alleyway, coughing and moaning and clearly in distress. The vast majority of those who thought they were in a hurry ignored the man. Some literally stepped over him.[3] The result was surprising; one might have expected those reflecting on the Good Samaritan to recognize that helping a stranger was, in the grand scheme of things, more important than being punctual for a seminar.

Still, at least a rationale of sorts could be offered for their conduct: it's not considerate to keep people waiting. But more recently there has been a plethora of studies showing that our ethical behavior appears to be linked to countless irrational or nonrational factors. For example, before mobile phones became ubiquitous, one American study showed that when subjects emerged from a public phone booth, they were much more likely to help a passer-by who dropped a pile of papers if they had first found a dime in the return slot of the phone. This nano-fragment of good fortune, of negligible monetary value, had a huge impact on how people acted. Yet another study proved that our behavior is affected by smell. We're more likely to be generous toward others if we're outside a bakery, breathing in the delicious aroma of baking bread. Whether the desk on which we're filling out a questionnaire is tidy and clean or messy with sticky stains can influence our answers to moral questions, such as opinions on crime and punishment. Scarily, the chance that a judge will rule that a prisoner be granted parole appears to depend on how long it's been since the judge's last meal.[4]

Although we like to fool ourselves into believing that we freely make decisions in the light of informed and reasoned reflection, the growing evidence from experimentation is that reason often takes a back seat to unconscious influences. Certainly our behavior is far more "situationist"—affected by a multitude of circumstances—than we might previously have imagined, and the research is a blow to the idea that character traits are stable and consistent, that the brave person will always be brave, the stingy person stingy, and the compassionate person compassionate. This has implications for government and education policy. Perhaps we should be focusing more on shaping conditions than character. As Anthony Appiah puts it: "Would you rather have people be helpful or not? It turns out that having little nice things happen to them is a much better way of making them helpful than spending a huge amount of energy on improving their characters."[5]

Three-dimensional Trolley

Trolleys have provided plenty of buffet-carriage fodder for psychologists. Philosophers have posed the trolley dilemmas in seminar rooms or on paper or on screen. But reading text on a screen doesn't even approximate to real-life situations.

So how could one ever engineer realistic trolley-like scenarios for unsuspecting subjects? Testing for real-life trolley reaction is not as straightforward as testing for a behavioral effect of the smell of baking bread or tinkering with the conditions that might influence people to help a stranger in distress.

This hasn't stopped ingenious psychology experimentalists from trying. A study conducted in 2011 placed subjects in a 3-D virtual-reality environment. In one scenario, the trolley was heading toward five and subjects could turn it to hit the one. In the other, the trolley was in any case en route to hitting the one and so subjects had nothing to do to avoid killing the five (although there was the option of turning the trolley so that it did hit the five). In an attempt to replicate reality, shrieks of distress became audible as the train careened toward those on the track. The study raised ethical issues of its own: several people were so disturbed by the experiment that they withdrew from it. In both cases, the vast majority of those who persisted with the experiment chose to kill or allow the one to die, to spare the five. But when positive action was required to save the five, subjects became more emotionally aroused than when they had to do nothing to achieve the same outcome.[6]

Psychologists have also altered other variables. One experiment divided subjects into two groups. Before the first group was exposed to the trolley problem they were shown a funny five-minute clip from the television show, *Saturday Night Live*. The second group had to sit through part of a tedious documentary about a Spanish village. Those who had been exposed to the comedy, and so (presumably) contemplating matters of life and death in a jaunty mood, were more likely to sanction the killing of the fat man.[7]

Our reactions can even be influenced by the name accorded the fat man, as another study revealed. Subjects were offered the choice between pushing "Tyrone Payton" (a stereotypical African American name) off the footbridge to save one hundred members of the New York Philharmonic and pushing "Chip Ellsworth III" (a name conjuring up white Anglo-Saxon old money) to save one hundred members of the Harlem Jazz Orchestra. The researchers discovered conservatives were indifferent between these options, but at the hands of liberals, aristocratic Chip fared less well than Tyrone. Perhaps liberals were bending over backward not to be racist—or perhaps Chip

Ellsworth III conjured up an image of wealth and privilege and they were motivated by egalitarian considerations (or, less charitably, envy?).[8]

Intriguingly, although only 10 percent of people would push the fat man, we tend to have far stronger utilitarian instincts when the dilemma is presented with animals instead of humans. Thus, one study asked subjects whether they would push a fat monkey off the footbridge to save five monkeys. The answer was "yes." People do not object to treating animals as means to a greater end. Our typical reflexes about animals are not Kantian but Benthamite.[9]

Janet and Jon

Although there are an infinite number of factors that might potentially influence our behavior and moral judgments, a consensus is emerging that there are two broad processes involved. Exactly how to characterize these two processes, and the balance of power between them, is contested territory. But the dichotomy, drawing on twenty-first century tools and methods, echoes a much older clash between the two most important philosophers of the eighteenth century—David Hume and Immanuel Kant. "Reason is, and ought only to be the slave of the passions," wrote Hume.[10] Kant held, on the contrary, that morality must be governed by reason.

In pioneering papers such as *The Emotional Dog and its Rational Tail*, the psychologist Jonathan Haidt argues that the emotions do much of the heavy lifting. Haidt has principally interrogated aspects of our morality that provoke disgust, or YUK! reactions. Take the imaginary scenario for which he is probably best known. Julie and Mark are siblings traveling in

France on summer vacation from college. One night they're staying alone in a cabin near the beach. They decide that it would be interesting and fun if they tried making love. At the very least, it would be a new experience for each of them. Julie is already taking birth control pills, but Mark uses a condom too, just to be safe. They both enjoy making love, but they decide never to do it again. They keep that night they slept together as a special secret, one that makes them feel even closer to each other.[11]

If you fail to find the idea of Julie and Mark having sex a bit yucky, well, at the very least you're in a small minority. Haidt found that, to varying degrees, almost everyone he questioned thought the siblings' behavior was morally reprehensible. But when he questioned people about why it was wrong, his subjects struggled to account for their feelings. Thus, they might first say that they were worried that any offspring from the sexual act might have genetic flaws, until reminded that there would be no offspring since two forms of contraception were used. Or they might raise concern at the long-term psychological impact, forgetting that for Julie and Mark the experience was an entirely positive one.

So here was an example in which nobody was harmed, and yet people still felt an immoral act had taken place: why it was wrong they somehow could not quite pinpoint. Baffled and frustrated, they ran out of explanation. They resorted to comments like, "Well, I just know in my gut it's wrong." Haidt gave this feeling a name: he labeled it "moral dumbfounding."[12]

In one experiment Haidt and a colleague used hypnosis to make people feel disgusted when an arbitrarily chosen word was used. That word was "often." They found that if a scenario was presented into which this word was slotted, hypnotized subjects judged any moral wrongdoing more harshly. More strikingly yet, a substantial minority still identified wrongdoing in situations where clearly there was none — such as the following. "Dan is a student council representative at his school. This semester he is in charge of scheduling discussions about academic issues. He often picks topics that appeal to both professors and students in order to stimulate discussion." When asked why they thought Dan had done something wrong, subjects would flounder around in a search of a response. "It just seems like he's up to something."[13]

In the 1970s there was a running gag in *Morecambe and Wise*, then Britain's most popular comedy television program. Eric Morecambe and Ernie Wise would perform a series of sketches, but then, right at the end, having played no previous part in the show, a large woman called Janet would stroll onto the stage wearing a ball gown. She would shove Eric and Ernie out of the way and announce, "I'd like to thank you for watching me and my little show." Jonathan Haidt sees reason as taking the role of Janet. It enters at the last minute, having done none of the work, and claims all the credit.

But, while Haidt believes that the emotions reign, others are not so sure: they view the clash between reason and emotion as a genuine tug of war.

Wrestling with Neurons

The heart has its reasons, of which
reason knows nothing.

—Pascal

Act that your principle of action might safely
be made a law for the whole world.

—Immanuel Kant

"You stand here in the dock, accused of killing a fat man. How do you plead?"

"Guilty, m'Lord. But in mitigation, my choice, my action, was determined by my brain, not by me."

"Your brain decides nothing. You decide. I sentence you to impudence and ten years of hard philosophy."

Lighting Up

In the past decade there has been an explosion of research into all aspects of the brain, driven by improvements in scanning technology. MRI (Magnetic Resonance Imaging) scans have yielded intriguing results. The scanners work by detecting minute variations in blood flow: when a particular part of the brain is engaged in more activity than in the so-called resting state it is shown, as neuroscientists put it, "lighting up." Research is in its infancy, but the evidence is becoming overwhelming that particular bits of the brain are of particular use for particular functions. Subjects lie inside the large (and noisy) tubes and scans are taken while, for example, they listen to music or use language or navigate maps or imagine themselves engaged in various physical activities, or observe faces or artworks or disgusting creatures and objects like cockroaches and feces.

What happens in the brain when we make moral decisions is also under investigation—and because the trolley dilemmas give rise to such competing intuitive tugs, they've proved among the most popular of case studies. The preeminent superstar in this area is Harvard psychologist and neuroscientist Joshua Greene.

Greene was a debater at school, one who was instinctively attracted to utilitarianism. When a discussion hinged on the relative significance of individual rights compared to the greater good, he'd adopt the Benthamite rather than the Kantian line. The consequences were what mattered. But he was flummoxed when first confronted with the transplant scenario: surely it couldn't be right to kill a healthy young man for use of his organs, even if this saved five lives. His utilitarian faith was shaken.

As a Harvard undergraduate he was introduced to the trolley problem—another baffling puzzle for a person of utilitarian persuasion. But, he says, it was only when he came across the peculiar case of Phineas P. Gage that he had his eureka moment. He was in Israel for his sister's bat mitzvah, reading a book in his hotel room.

The Crowbar Case

Phineas Gage was a twenty-five-year-old construction foreman who would become a real, rather than hypothetical, victim of the railways. His job was to coordinate a group of workers who were building a railway track across Vermont. To make the route as direct as possible, the team would on occasion have to force an opening through rock. At 4:30 one summer afternoon there was a catastrophic accident. A fuse was lit prematurely. There was a massive blast, and the iron rod used to cram down the explosive powder shot into Gage's cheek, went through the front of his brain, and exited via the top of his head.

That Gage was not killed instantly was miraculous. More miraculous still was that within a couple of months he seemed to be physically almost back to normal. His limbs functioned and he could see, feel, and talk. But it's what happened next that transformed him from a medical curiosity into an academic case study. Although he was physically able to operate much as before, it became apparent that his character had been transformed—for the worse. Where he had once been responsible and self-controlled, now he was impulsive, capricious, and unreliable. It's difficult to separate myth from reality, but one report says his tongue became so vulgar that the fairer and more delicate sex were strongly urged to avoid his company.

In his book, *Descartes' Error*, the neuroscientist Antonio Damasio says Gage could know but not feel.[1] "This is it!" thought Greene, in his hotel room. "That's what's happening in the Footbridge and transplant cases. We *feel* that we shouldn't push the fat man. But we *think* it better to save five rather than one life. And the feeling and the thought are distinct."

137

Trained in both philosophy and psychology, Greene was the first person to throw neuroscience into the trolley mix. He began to scan subjects while they were presented with trolley problems: the scanners picked up where blips in the resulting brain activity took place.

Greene describes the trolley cases as triggering a furious bout of neural wrestling between the calculating and emotional bits of the brain. It's a much more evenly fought tussle than that described by Haidt. Presented with the Fat Man dilemma, and the option of killing with your bare hands, parts of the brain situated just behind the eyes and thought to be crucial to feelings such as compassion (the amygdala, the posterior cingulate cortex, and the medial prefrontal cortex), move into overdrive. The idea of pushing the fat man "sets off an emotional alarm bell in your brain that makes you say 'no, that's wrong'."[2] Without that metaphorical alarm, we default to a utilitarian calculus: the calculating part of the brain (the dorsolateral prefrontal cortex and inferior parietal lobe) assesses costs and benefits of various kinds, not just moral costs and benefits. In Spur, the equation is not complicated: at the cost of one life we can benefit five.

A camera provides the basis for another helpful Greene metaphor. A camera has automatic settings—a setting for landscapes, say. That's useful because it saves time. We see something we want to photograph and we press a button. But sometimes we want to mess around, try something fresh and unusual, be a bit arty and avant-garde. Perhaps we want the central image to be fuzzy. The only way we can achieve that effect is to switch to manual (calculating) mode. "Emotional responses are like the automatic responses on your camera. The flexible kind of action planning, that's manual mode."[3]

The emotional parts of the brain are believed to have evolved long before the brain regions responsible for analysis and planning. In a moral dilemma one might therefore expect emotion to race more quickly to a conclusion than reason. Studies have shown that forcing people to go fast makes them less utilitarian.[4]

That there appears to be a fight between two settings is nicely corroborated by a study involving what researchers call "cognitive load." While subjects were considering the trolley problems, their cognitive processes were simultaneously engaged in another task—typically looking at (or adding) numbers that flash up on a screen. Under such conditions, subjects were slower to give the utilitarian answer, to kill the one to save the five in Spur (when the cognitive processes are engaged), but the task made no difference in the Fat Man dilemma, which principally engages the emotions.

The emotional recoiling that typically occurs when people contemplate killing the fat man is made up, Greene says, of two components. The first is an up-close-and-personal effect: there is something about the physicality of pushing, the direct impacting of another person with one's muscles, that makes us flinch. The evidence suggests that this is even the case if the pushing doesn't directly require contact with hands, but is achieved with a long pole that nonetheless uses similar muscles. The effect can be tested in the Trap Door case.

In the Trap Door scenario, we can stop the train and save the five lives by turning a switch (much like the switch in Spur). This switch opens a trap door on which the fat man happens to be standing. Now, while the most casuistically minded lawyer would be unable to identify any substantial moral distinction between killing with a switch and killing with a push,

Figure 10. *The Trap Door.* The runaway trolley is heading toward five people. You are standing by the side of the track. The only way to stop the trolley killing the five is to pull a lever which opens a trap door on which a fat man happens to be standing. The fat man would plummet to the ground and die, but his body would stop the trolley. Should you open the trap door?

subjects asked about the trolley cases are more willing to send the fat man to his death when it involves the former rather than the latter. Still, whether it requires a switch or a push, most people still believe that killing the fat man is worse than changing the train's direction in Spur.

Which means there must be something else going on too . . .

The second factor, says Greene, syncs nicely with the Doctrine of Double Effect. We are more reluctant to harm someone intentionally, as a means to a desired end, than to harm them merely as a side effect. These two factors—physical contact and intent to harm—"have no or little impact separately, but when you combine them they produce an effect that's much bigger than the sum of the separate effects. It's like a drug interaction, where if you take Drug A you're fine, and if you take Drug B you're fine, but take them both together and BAM!"[5] Pushing the fat man, which combines a physical act with an intention to harm, produces this emotional BAM!

Evolutionary Errors

Greene has a compelling, if speculative, evolutionary explanation for the strange moral distinction people subconsciously draw between engaging muscles and turning switches. We have a particular revulsion to harms that could have been inflicted in the environment of our evolutionary adaptation. We evolved in environments in which we interacted directly with other human beings—force had to come from one's own muscles. Using muscles to shove another person is a cue that there's violence involved and for obvious reasons violence is generally best avoided.

These experiments focus on moral judgment, rather than behavior, on how people actually act. However, judgment and behavior are linked. And whether or not we buy into Greene's evolutionary story, the psychology of killing has profound significance beyond the academic realm of trolleyology. The skies over Pakistan and Afghanistan are regularly crisscrossed by unmanned U.S. aircraft, drones, operated from thousands of miles away in the United States, usually by relatively young men. Up to 2,680 people may have been killed by U.S. drones in Pakistan alone in the seven years prior to 2011.[6] Drones represent the future of warfare: currently some drones are used for reconnaissance, while others target people and buildings. Whether we find it easier to kill by moving a joystick or by puncturing a throat with a bayonet is by itself a morally neutral discovery. After all, if we face a deadly enemy we may want our soldiers to feel less compunction about killing. But if it's true, as it seems to be, that we can more easily kill by flicking a switch than by thrusting with a bayonet, then that's something we need to know about.

This debate fits into a wider discussion about how well (or badly) evolution has equipped us ethically for the modern age. Philosophers, particularly of a utilitarian persuasion, have highlighted the following apparent inconsistency. If we walked past a shallow pond and saw a young child drowning, most of us would instinctively jump straight in to rescue her. We would do so even if we were wearing expensive clothes. We would be outraged by an observer who stood idly by as the child thrashed about and who later explained that she couldn't possibly have plunged in because she was wearing her favorite Versace skirt that had cost $500. Yet few of us respond to letters from charities who point out that similar amounts of money could save lives on the far side of the world.

There doesn't seem to be an obvious ethical difference between saving a stranger in front of us and saving one far away. But there's a plausible evolutionary explanation for our contrasting reactions. The modern human brain evolved when humans were hunter-gatherers, living in small groups of between 100 and 150. It was of benefit (in evolutionary terms) to care for our offspring and the few others with whom we cooperated. We didn't want or need to know about what was happening on the far side of the mountain, valley, or lake. Technology now brings us instant news of catastrophes elsewhere in the world. That we're so uncharitable in responding to such events is hardly surprising—even if it's morally indefensible. Peter Singer gives the following trolleyesque example:

> Suppose that we are in a boat in a storm and we see two capsized yachts. We can either rescue one person clinging to one upturned yacht, or five people whom we cannot see, but we know are trapped inside the other upturned yacht. We will have time to go to only one of the yachts before they are pounded onto the rocks and, most likely, anyone clinging to the yacht we do not go to will be drowned. We can identify the man who is alone—we know his name and what he looks like, although otherwise we know nothing about him and have no connection with him. We don't know anything about who is trapped inside the other yacht, except that there are five of them.[7]

Countless studies show how our moral decisions—such as how much charity we donate to a cause, or how harsh we think a punishment should be—are significantly influenced by whether we can identify the person or persons affected by our actions.[8] But surely, says Singer of his example, we should save the five—even if evolution has, as it were, inveigled us into caring more about the victim we can identify. And we need to draw an obvious conclusion from Singer's scenario: some of our moral instincts are inappropriate for our age, an era in which people live in large, anonymous groups in an interconnected world.

The forces of evolution have shaped our moral instincts in another sense. Evolution has provided us with heuristics—rules of thumb—about how we should behave. Rules of thumb are convenient since we do not have infinite time, money, or information to work out what to do on each occasion. They're useful to navigate complexity, and decision making is routinely complex. But although heuristics may work for us in the majority of occasions, they can also let us down. For one thing, as already discussed,[9] rules may conflict, so we need a procedure for resolving clashes. "Save lives" and "Do not lie" will clash if we have to lie to save lives. Moreover, sometimes a rule will use a cue, or signal, or proxy, and this can produce both false positives and negatives. Take the heuristic rule against incest: there are rational medical and biological reasons not to reproduce with a sibling. Evolution appears to have given us a rule of thumb that discourages incest: do not find sexually attractive another person with whom you've been raised. It's a rule that has served us well. But it might lead to problems when siblings are separated in childhood and find each other attractive when they meet later in life, and it has caused a crisis in the kibbutzim in Israel, where children from different families are raised communally and grow up feeling little sexual attraction to one another—with a low rate of marriage within the kibbutzim as a consequence.[10]

Farewell Freedom

At one level it's scarcely surprising that the scientist can contribute to the Fat Man dilemma in particular and to the understanding of morality in general. Of course there is a link between the brain and morality. It is impossible to conceive how it could be otherwise. Our behavior and our beliefs have to be the product in part of our neural circuitry. Without brains there could be no beliefs.

But what's new is our growing understanding of how the architecture and engineering works, which bits of the brain do what, and how they are connected. It's a debate that is relevant to the encroachment of neuroethics into the law. In the future, we can expect more pleas of mitigation of the form, "it wasn't me, it was my brain." Our system of justice rests on the notion that humans are free to act, free to choose. We don't hold a person responsible for an action that they were forced to perform. And the more we discover about the brain, and the more we can explain and predict action, the smaller and smaller becomes the space available for the operation of free will—or so it might seem.

However, "compatibilists" maintain that free will is consistent with a full causal explanation of our thoughts and actions. Even if a gigantic computer programmed with zillions of bytes of data could accurately predict a person's actions, that wouldn't imply—insists the compatibilist—that action was not free. This seems a puzzling claim, to me at least, though the compatibilist position on free will is probably the most popular among philosophers writing on this subject. But whatever position one adopts in this perennial debate, it's inevitable that the courts will increasingly be asked to take into account biologically grounded excuses and pleas for mitigation based on brain scans and medical evidence.

Consider the example of a predatory sexual harasser in the year 2000. This middle-aged American male had spent years happily married, exhibiting no unusual sexual proclivities. Almost overnight he developed an interest in prostitution and child pornography. His wife became aware of this, and when he began making advances toward his stepdaughter, she informed the authorities. Her husband was found guilty of child molestation and sentenced to rehabilitation. That did nothing to discourage him: he carried on harassing women at the center where he was undergoing his rehabilitation. A jail sentence seemed inevitable.

For some time he had been beset by headaches, and these were becoming more intense. Just hours before his sentencing he went to the hospital, where a brain scan revealed a massive tumor. Once this was removed, his conduct returned to normal. That could have been the end of the story, but six months later the wildly inappropriate behavior started up again. The man went back to the doctors. It turned out that a part of the tumor had been missed in the first operation and had now expanded. A second operation was entirely successful and had an instantaneous effect on the patient's aberrant sexuality. The man was spared jail.

A tumor is an extreme example. Few would hold a person responsible for his actions if such a growth had radically altered his decision making. But in the future, neuroscientists will point to other physical causes that we don't currently categorize under terms like "disease," "illness," or "condition." A neuroscientist might say, "Mary's shoplifting can be explained by the chemical composition and synapses in her brain." It's not obvious why this excuse would be, in theory, any less convincing than one that references a tumor.[11]

One important means by which neuroscientists are learning about the relationship between the brain and ethics is through atypical cases, arising from accidental lesions and disease. Although neuroethics is a niche area, the emerging picture of ethics has similarities to that being drawn by specialists in other parts of the brain, be it language, the senses, face recognition, the relationship between the brain and the body, or consciousness. The brain is a delicate, intricate, interlinked construction, in precarious equilibrium, and the absence or removal or mis-wiring of one tiny piece of the engineering can produce weird phenomena and curious behavior.

Capgras syndrome is the perfect illustration. Capgras is a condition in which a person believes that his wife or father or close friend has been replaced by an imposter. In the past those making such a claim were quickly labeled insane. But neuroscientists like Vilayanur Ramachandran, intrigued by such cases, sought a physiological explanation—and came up with a simple one. Most of us are superb at recognizing faces and storing information about them: if asked, we may not be able to articulate how the faces of two brothers differ, but in their presence we have no trouble telling them apart. This vital skill appears to depend on the normal functioning of a particular part of the brain called the fusiform gyrus. Damage to this area can lead to prosopagnosia, a condition in which patients cannot distinguish faces. According to Ramachandran, patients with Capgras syndrome have normally functioning face recognition, but there is some kind of transmission problem connecting the fusiform gyrus to the limbic system, central to our emotional life. The absence of any emotional kick when Capgras sufferers see a person with their mother's face leads them to conclude that this person is some kind of charlatan.[12]

Dual Systems

The typical ethical outlook of the typical human being relies on a balance of neural systems.

Joshua Greene initially saw the opposition as one between emotion and calculation, Haidt between emotion and reason (and in his more recent work, between automaticity/intuition and reason), Daniel Kahneman, the Nobel Prize–winning psychologist, between fast and slow systems.[13]

These dual systems need not be entirely independent of one another. Thus, even if, as Haidt insists, emotion is in the driver's seat, reason might have acted in an earlier and influential role as driving instructor. For example, in most of the developed world, homosexuality doesn't repulse people in the way that it used to—so people are less likely to judge it wrong. But reason, presumably, played at least some role in altering the social norm that found homosexuality disgusting.[14]

Many of those working on the science of morality believe that their findings have normative import. Thus Haidt says that in his incest scenario, people should overcome their emotional Yuk! reaction—reason tells us that there can be no objection to a relationship between two consenting adults where no harm is done. And Greene argues that our automatic responses to situations—though hugely useful—can also misfire, and that in moral dilemmas our calculating side should take primacy: we should shift into manual mode. We should push the fat man, despite our instinctive abhorrence of doing so. Peter Singer agrees: if resistance to pushing the fat man is driven by the brain's emotional mechanisms, we should overcome our squeamishness.[15]

Some people have little or no squeamishness. What makes some people more utilitarian than others is now under investigation. People who are good at visual imagery have weaker utilitarian instincts (presumably the image of killing the fat man strikes them with greater force).[16] If subjects are forced to think longer about a problem, their judgment will be more utilitarian than if they have to give an instant response.[17]

That emotions are linked to the frontal lobe of the brain has been known at least since the iron rod transformed Phineas P. Gage. We can have a guess at what Phineas Gage's post-accident reaction would have been to the imaginary rail disasters in trolleyology. In the past few years, studies have been carried out on people with damage to the ventromedial prefrontal cortex.[18] Such patients are more blasé about the fate of the fat man. Damaged patients are about twice as likely as normal people to say that it's acceptable to push the fat man to his death to save other lives. There are similar findings when patients are asked some heart-stopping cases discussed earlier, such as the parents hiding from the Nazis who must suffocate their child to prevent the entire group being discovered and killed. Damaged patients feel less internal conflict than the healthy: that suffocating the child is the right thing to do seems more obvious to them. They have a reduced emotional response to causing harm.

There are also related studies on psychopaths. Psychopaths, and those with psychopathic traits, tend to be more likely than others to endorse direct harm in trolley-like scenarios.[19] Some psychologists have turned their specialist eye on rigid utilitarians like Jeremy Bentham: one paper posits that his moral outlook is linked to a diagnosis of Asperger's Syndrome.[20]

It's not easy working out the implications of these studies for morality. If there is a link between a certain type of brain damage and utilitarianism, are we to infer that sometimes brain-damaged patients have clearer moral vision than others? Or should we instead take such findings as evidence that there is something not fully rounded about utilitarianism—and that those who advocate the pushing of the fat man have a fundamental flaw in their ethical apparatus? The latter is at least plausible. Since psychopaths are poor at judging what is right in certain uncontentious cases, it seems reasonable to conclude that their judgment is also suspect in trolley cases. In other words, the fact that psychopaths are more likely to endorse the killing of the fat man provides weak evidence that killing the fat man is wrong.

Neurobabble

Neuroscience is muscling in on many disciplines. It is new, exciting, and producing fascinating results. But it has fierce critics, particularly when it purports to shed light on ethics. One line of attack is that it is flawed methodologically: that it is poor science.

Brain-scanning is indeed still a crude tool with crude measurements. And gauging the response of subjects while they are lying prone in a long tube can hardly replicate any real-life dilemma. However deeply the patients immerse themselves in the dilemma, however successful they are in imagining themselves inside it, in suspending disbelief, they're unlikely to feel the thumping heart, the sweaty palms, the fear, panic, and anxiety of real life. The ordinary sounds, smells, and sights are absent. There is no chatter or rumbling street noise in the background, no raindrops or sunshine.[21]

The point is not that sunshine *ought* to affect our decisions. Whether or not I donate to drought victims on the far corner of the globe should not depend on how my mood is altered by the weather. But real life does contain multiple influencing factors, so we should be wary of extrapolating from the white tube to real life.

But there's a more fundamental objection to the claims of neuroscience. The gravamen of the charge is that there's some sort of category error involved. The twentieth-century British philosopher, Gilbert Ryle, who introduced the notion of the category error, illustrated it with the example of the American tourist who arrived at Oxford and, after seeing the Sheldonian theater, the Bodleian library, and the colleges and quads, innocently asked, "But where is the University?" as though the university were somehow a separate physical entity.

The related thought is that ascribing ideas, choices and motives, desires and prejudices, to the brain is some sort of category error. Ryle was influenced by Wittgenstein, and many critics of neuroscience are themselves Wittgensteinians. The Wittgensteinian critique of neuroscience is that psychological attributes cannot be ascribed to brains; they can only be ascribed to human beings. The mind, they say, is not identical to the brain. I can be confused (in two minds) about whether to turn the trolley. My brain is not confused. I can recoil at the thought of using physical force to kill a fat man. My brain cannot be aghast at such a prospect. I can calculate that it is better to lose one life rather than five: it makes no sense to say my brain does this calculation. Of course, if my brain didn't function, I wouldn't function, but that's not to say that I am identical to my brain. A train wouldn't function without an engine, but the train is not identical to the engine.[22]

But for the most part the neuroskeptics are throwing feather darts at straw men. On the whole, when neuroscientists talk about the brain being confused, or aghast, they are speaking metaphorically.[23] The neuroskeptic then charges the neuroscientist with another error. The neuroskeptic says that behavior is best understood not by peering into a brain, but by situating a person in the environment. But this too is a feeble missile. For only the crassest scientist claims that brain activity is the single or the best explanation for human behavior and conscious states, or that it's any substitute at all for other types of explanation. It is indeed silly to say that a description of being in love, or an explanation for a person's political ideology, could be located in a particular area of the brain. Love and politics can't be reduced to some sort of chemical commotion. A brain is situated in a body. And people belong to cultures and societies. An answer to why a person voted Democrat or Republican cannot be confined to an account of the neural pinball at work between the ears.

Nonetheless, being in love and having a particular political ideology are impossible without the brain, and neuroscientists are now discovering fascinating correlations between some acts, beliefs, and feelings and neurological activity, evidence that can't be dismissed. As we've seen, an injury to the ventro-medial prefrontal cortex can alter moral judgment. We also now understand that the prefrontal cortex is involved in inhibition—and if it is eroded by, say, dementia, sufferers might end up "shoplifting in front of store managers, removing their clothes in public, running stop signs, breaking out in song at inappropriate times, eating food scraps found in public trash cans. . . ."[24] Equally, neuroscientists are discovering more about the chemicals that drive abnormal and destructive behavior, like addiction, be it to food, gambling, sex, or shopping. The neurotransmitter, dopamine, is a key player here. There have been many tragic cases of sufferers with Parkinson's disease being treated with dopaminergic medications and then being unable to control their impulses, costing them their savings, careers, and marriages.

This raises the intriguing possibility that we ourselves could begin to tamper with the brain to alter our moral outlook—and thus alter our judgments in the trolley cases. . . .

Bionic Trolley

You do look glum! What you need
is a gramme of soma.

—*Aldous Huxley,* Brave New World

The best way to find out if you can
trust somebody is to trust them.

—*Ernest Hemingway*

IF JEREMY BENTHAM RULED the world he would encourage the toppling of fat men over footbridges, where this sacrifice was necessary for the greater good. But ordinary folk can't bring themselves to push the fat man. Ordinary folk don't believe that their primary obligation is to maximize happiness; they believe that there are constraints on their behavior, such as a prohibition on harming innocent individuals. Even if they were persuaded by Jeremy Bentham, and did push the fat man, they'd probably feel terrible remorse afterward: perhaps they'd suffer flashbacks and nightmares. Bentham would no doubt regard any guilt or regret as irrational. But humans aren't always in control of their emotions. Striving to be utilitarian might have the perverse effect of making us unhappy.

Fortunately, help from the laboratory is now at hand. Scientists are learning more and more about how memory works. The hippocampus (the size of a little finger and so-called because it loosely resembles a sea horse) is the area of the brain that is thought to cement memory, arranging and ordering beliefs and images. The almond-shaped amygdala signals to the hippocampus which memories it is important to store. The more intense the emotional arousal in the amygdala, the more likely a memory is to be retained.

Evolution, as usual, is to be congratulated for coming up with a thoroughly pragmatic arrangement. We forget most things that have happened to us. But if we're attacked by a stranger in the street, we need to ensure that we remember this menacing episode: we don't want to find ourselves in a similarly perilous situation again. Sometimes such an episode causes an overreaction: the emotional impact of what we experience is so intense that it blows a memory fuse. This seems to be what occurs with Post Traumatic Stress Disorder (PTSD), a condition long taken seriously by the military. PTSD sufferers are constantly reminded of the harrowing event. Their memories might be triggered, say, by the bang of an exhaust pipe (sounding like an explosion of a shell) as well as by more tenuous links to the traumatic episode. A soldier who witnessed a friend shot in a trench might have a panic attack on seeing a muddy field.

Some time ago, researchers found out that if within a few hours of a disturbing episode, subjects took propranolol, a beta-blocker, they were less likely to develop PTSD. More recent studies show that propranolol can assist even those who have suffered PTSD for years. Memory specialists use an analogy to explain the drug's impact. Imagine that you order a book in a library. The book is collected from the stacks. If you read it by an open window with the sun streaming in, the book will become slightly bleached. When you hand the book back, what gets stored is a fainter copy. Propranolol operates like aggressive bleaching sunlight. If subjects with PTSD are prompted to conjure up the unwelcome recurring memory while being injected with the drug, then the memory is restacked in the brain in a weakened state.

So in theory, even if we were squeamish about pushing the fat man, drugs might soon be available to allow us to emasculate the memory of doing so. But there may be a more direct way to influence our approach to the trolley problem—a pill not to dull the trauma, but to modify our values.

The Moral Dispensary

Science will soon offer up a giddying smorgasbord of enhancement possibilities: physical enhancement, cognitive enhancement, mood enhancement. Some drugs are already available. For decades, cheating athletes have turned to chemical/biological performance boosters to improve a range of physical skills—and such drugs and medical interventions are becoming increasingly targeted and sophisticated. The same is true for cognitive enhancement. Coffee drinkers have long known about the restorative qualities of caffeine. But as neuroscientists discover more about how we learn languages, read music, identify patterns, focus on tasks, memorize facts, and multiply numbers, so there will inevitably be pills designed for ever more specific functions.

The idea of mood enhancement pills smacks of a *Brave New World*. In Aldous Huxley's futuristic novel (published in 1932), soma keeps everyone in a state of subdued contentment. The reader feels that the hallucinogen is an agent of control, and makes the lives of those who consume it inauthentic and divorced from reality. Yet beer drinkers have long known about the swift and impressive impact of lager and ale on mood and inhibition, and drugs like Prozac, prescribed for depression, have become so ubiquitous in parts of the developed world that there's barely any social stigma attached to their use.

Even more contentious than mood-changing, however, is moral "improvement." The influence of parents, in particular, but also friends, teachers, and society more widely, remains the most effective lever on attitudes and behavior. That will not always necessarily be the case. Our knowledge of the chemical and biological underpinnings involved in our ethical evaluations is nascent but rapidly progressing. We're beginning to understand the role and impact of natural chemicals such as oxytocin, testosterone, vasopressin, serotonin, and dopamine. By tampering with the quantities absorbed in the human body, psychologists, doctors, and philosophers are discovering how these chemicals alter behavior, how they change attitudes toward risk, toward negotiation, bargaining, and cooperation, toward impulse control and reward gratification. Even toward breeding and sex.

If you want to learn about the birds and the bees, one useful place to start is the prairie vole. These rodents, with their stout bodies and hairy tails, are not the most alluring creatures, at least seen through human eyes. But, fortunately for the survival of their species, the male and female prairie voles find each other more fetching. Indeed, once they've identified a mate, they remain in apparently blissful union, sexually faithful, for the duration of their short lives.

The prairie vole has a near cousin, the meadow vole. The male meadow vole differs in one particular: he is highly promiscuous, a bit of a love rat. It transpires that when the prairie vole mates, a hormone called vasopressin is released, and the cells that respond to the vasopressin—the receptors—are located in the pleasure areas of the brain. The mating partner of the prairie vole is a cause of the pleasure, and thus a bond between the pair is formed. With meadow moles, however, the receptors are in a different part of the brain, so mating doesn't produce the same compulsion to pair. But by introducing a single new gene, one that influences vasopressin receptors, scientists managed to convert male meadow voles into loyal lovers.

When it comes to love and sex, humans and voles seem to have a lot in common. A study of Swedish twin brothers found that differences in the way that the hormone vasopressin was absorbed correlated strongly with how well each man fared in marriage, assessed by levels of infidelity and divorce. It is not overly fanciful to imagine that one day we may demand that our partners be tested for the hormone, or farther into the future, even use gene therapy to foster sexual fidelity.

That's sex. Can we also modify attitudes to another intractable divider of society: race? Propranolol, the beta-blocker discussed above, has a variety of curious effects over and above its impact on memory. There's a test anybody can take, the Implicit Attitude Test, in which certain words, nice words (such as peace, laughter, pleasure) and nasty words (evil, failure, hurt) have to be attached to black and white faces. Most people want to believe they're not racist and are likely to find their results disconcerting. The IAT shows that we carry around with us varying degrees of subconscious racial bias: we're quicker to associate nasty words with black faces than with white. And black people themselves tend to exhibit the same bias. But if we're given propranolol before taking the test, much of the implicit bias disappears.[1]

Changing ethical behavior and judgment with chemicals is no longer an option restricted to the world of sci-fi novelists. And how people react to the trolley scenarios when taking them has proved a useful indicator of whether and how certain chemicals can transform their moral convictions. The impact of propranolol on judgments in trolley scenarios is still unclear.[2] But experimentalists have modified various hormones and in so doing altered responses: for example, one study adjusted levels of serotonin in the body. It found that increasing levels of serotonin made people less utilitarian, less willing to push the fat man.

But the trolley problem is not the only test available to scientists wanting to determine how they can modulate our morality. Another involves the division of a fistful of dollars.

The Ultimatum Game

The Pullman Strike in the United States in the nineteenth century is typical of many strikes. It was colossally expensive for the Pullman Company and a disaster for the union and its members. The strike cost the railroads alone nearly around $4.5 million in lost revenue and another $700,000 in expenses. The 100,000 striking employees lost wages worth an estimated $1.4 million.

The phrase "win-win," which derives from Game Theory, has entered popular parlance. The phrase "lose-lose-lose" has not. But lose-lose-lose was the Pullman outcome: it's often the outcome of strikes. Companies lose. Workers lose. Invariably, the public loses too. It might be regarded as irrational for unions to pursue an approach that makes them worse off. Well, maybe so, at least under one definition of rationality. But in such matters humans are not always rational creatures—as an experiment in a basement in Queen Square at London University has investigated.

Picture the scene. There are two apparently thirsty men. Let's call them Harry and Olly. Harry and Olly have never met. They are offered a beaker of water to share. The first man, Harry, divides the water into two glasses. Into his glass he pours three-quarters of the beaker: into Olly's glass he decants the remaining quarter. Olly looks a little annoyed. But he's been given a choice. He can drink the amount Harry's offered him or he can reject it. If he rejects it, neither man gets anything to drink.

Olly has spent the past hour attached to a saline drip: his head aches a little, his mouth is dry, and any water is better than no water. But he looks at Harry's almost full glass of cool refreshment, then at his own measly amount, and he shakes his head: he'll be damned if he'll allow Harry to take almost all the drink for himself.

Harry, it turns out, is a plant. Unbeknown to him, Olly has been tested on a puzzle with many parallels to the trolley problem: the Ultimatum Game.[3]

The Ultimatum Game has had a career trajectory similar to the Fat Man's. It first appeared in 1982, shortly before the Fat Man. It began in one discipline (economics) and was analyzed as an idealized form of negotiation initially purely in an a priori way, a puzzle that could be resolved on paper with (quite simple) mathematics. The "solution" was then tested in the real world. After that the game flew the nest of its parent discipline and into other fields, including evolutionary biology, anthropology, sociology, and neuroscience. As with the Fat Man, findings from the Ultimatum Game have been cited as evidence that morality is hardwired, innate. As with the Fat Man, the game is being used to test how chemical intervention can alter decision making. And as with the Fat Man, there are vitriolic critics who condemn this academic construct for being an artificial laboratory experiment that cannot be transplanted in any useful way into the real world.

The standard Ultimatum Game involves two players. This time let's call them Thomas and Adam. Thomas is given a sum of money, say £100. He can then choose to give any amount of that £100 to Adam. Adam has the option of accepting this division of the £100 or rejecting it: if he rejects it, neither player receives anything. If Thomas offers only £1 to Adam, then it seems to make sense for Adam to accept it. If Adam accepts this distribution, he gets £1. £1 is better than nothing and nothing is what he will receive if he rejects the offer. Since it would make sense for Adam to accept any amount, however small, it would also seem to make sense for Thomas to offer the smallest possible amount.

That is the result that a mathematical model might predict: it's how some economists claim Rational Economic Man ought to respond. But, as it turns out, it's not how flesh-and-blood men and women react. When it was initially put to subjects in the United States, there were two surprises. First, those in the role of Thomas typically offered around 40 percent of the total pot: some even offered half. Second, those playing Adam, on the receiving end, typically rejected any offer that was below about 25 percent. They preferred to scotch the whole deal rather than accept what they regarded as a measly and insulting proposal.

The Ultimatum Game has become the economist's favorite experiment, conducted innumerable times. As with the Fat Man, experimenters have tinkered with the variables, testing it with different stakes, on different ages, on both sexes, on twins, between different races and groups, in different places, even on animals (chimpanzees are rational maximizers, taking whatever they're offered!)[4] There has been a comparison of behavior when the responder was plain-looking and when the responder was attractive. Another comparison has analyzed what happens when subjects know one another and when they're strangers. They've tried the Ultimatum Game on people who are exhausted and, as in the experiment with Harry and Olly, when people are thirsty.

To make the game feel real, the stakes have to be real. But funds are limited even in enviably endowed universities. So through financial necessity, the game has had to be played with small sums. That, of course, skews the findings, since if the comfortably well off are irked by a stingy offer, it's not too much of a hardship for them to snub it. But Ultimatum Game experiments have now been carried out in more than thirty countries, in places where the dollar has considerably more purchasing power than in the United States. The most extraordinary result was in Indonesia. In a $100 game, offers of $30 or lower were still routinely turned down. This was back in 1995 when $30 was the equivalent of a fortnight's wages.

So what's going on here? Why do people offer more than they need to and why are some offers rejected? Why would anyone scoff at free money?

There are two types of answer. In one camp are those who regard the results as misleading because they mask our basic naked self-interest. In the other are those who use the Ultimatum Game as evidence that we are at least partially altruistic and that we emerge from the womb with an ingrained belief in, and capacity for, fairness.

The Ultimatum Game is relatively new, but it taps into an argument with a long and impressive pedigree about, crudely put, whether humans are born good or evil (or whether they're shaped entirely by experience). Jesus Christ, John Locke, Jean-Jacques Rousseau, and the novelist William Golding have all contributed to this debate. Locke thought the mind at birth was a *tabula rasa*, a blank slate. Our beliefs were formed and molded by experience. But others—let's categorize them into the Hobbesians and the Smithians—suspected that a baby emerged from the womb with moral dispositions. Thomas Hobbes (1588–1679) believed that man was an essentially self-interested creature, and without a community or state police force, people would club one another to death. They would be scared even to go to sleep. While today's caricature of the Scottish economist and philosopher Adam Smith (1723–1790) has him endorsing this grim Hobbesian diagnosis of the human psyche, in fact the opposite was the case. True, Smith writes in *The Wealth of Nations* that the invisible hand of the market works well when people pursue personal gain. "It is not from the benevolence of the butcher, the brewer, or the baker, that we can expect our dinner but from their regard to their own interest."[5] Yet in *The Theory of Moral Sentiments* he explicitly states that self-interest is not the sole and dominating motivation: "How selfish soever man may be supposed, there are evidently some principles in his nature, which interest him in the fortunes of others, and render their happiness necessary to him, though he derives nothing from it, except the pleasure of seeing it."[6]

Both sides can cite Ultimatum Game studies to bolster their case. In an experiment in which the proposers were offered complete anonymity, many more people made greedy offers, suggesting that what seems to motivate people is not altruism but reputation. A good reputation for, say, honesty and fair dealing obviously lubricates transactions and negotiations. (Many of the studies have been carried out with students, who know that the professor is taking an interest in the results: hardly surprising, then, that they seek to ingratiate themselves by making generous offers.)

There's even cross-cultural support for the Hobbesian view. Although people in Indonesia behaved like those in Indiana, some quirky results were recorded elsewhere. In small-scale societies generous offers to strangers were less likely (possibly because in such societies there's normally no need to trade with strangers). What's more, in one or two remote parts of the world, in particular among the Au and Gnau peoples of Melanesia, there were examples of people making hyper-generous offers (in excess of 50 percent), and, more unusual still, seeing some of these offers rebuffed! This startling phenomenon was explained by researchers in terms of the Melanesian culture of status-seeking through the giving of gifts. Refusing a gift is a rejection of being subordinate. So these results are consistent with the Hobbesian analysis that we're fundamentally self-interested.

But there is also a heavy burden of evidence in support of the Smithians, that we're born altruistic, at least to a degree, and that it's our biology, an innate altruism or sense of justice, that drives us to make generous offers and an innate sense of fairness that compels us to reject bad ones. Certainly there seems to be evidence that biology plays a part. A study contrasting identical twins with fraternal twins in Sweden suggests a striking genetic factor: unlike fraternal twins, identical twins offered and accepted similar amounts.

Biological factors have been examined in other ways. When thirsty subjects were offered a poor distribution of water they often chose to go without rather than accept the deal. There have been experiments on subjects deprived of sleep. You might expect people who were tired to accept any offer they were given; that a mild state of discomfort would make people care less whether or not an offer was fair. In fact the opposite seems to occur. When people are deprived of sleep, and too tired to think reflectively about an offer, emotion predominates: a poor split is more likely to be hurled back into the proposer's face.

The same psychologists and neuroscientists who are investigating how we respond to the Trolley Problem also make use of the Ultimatum Game. Thus, there have been Ultimatum Game tests conducted both with psychopaths and with those who have damage to the ventromedial prefrontal cortex (which is involved in the formation of social emotions). As described earlier (see chapter 13), VMPC patients are more likely to push the Fat Man. When playing the Ultimatum Game, such patients are more likely to reject unfair offers. When frustrated or provoked, VMPC patients are prone to exhibit anger or petulance.

What happens in the brain when stingy (or generous) offers are made has been the focus of study by neuroscientists. The reward regions of the brain (associated, for example, with eating a chocolate bar) are more active when a recipient is offered a high amount, while the insula cortex, which responds to disgust, is activated when people are offered a small amount.

Pay Cheese

Just as researchers have used the trolley problems to assess the impact on behavior of hormones such as serotonin, testosterone, and oxytocin, the Ultimatum Game has served the same function.

Thus, an experiment showed that people with high levels of serotonin are more likely to accept offers that others regard as unfair. If you have to negotiate with union leaders over beer and sandwiches, a good tactic is to slip chunky slices of cheese between the bread: cheese is rich in serotonin. Workers who believe their managers are skimming most of the profits for themselves *will* consider cutting off their nose to spite their face, if they can simultaneously give a black eye to the bosses. They will, in other words, be inclined to hurt themselves if this is the only way to inflict punishment on others. But serotonin reduces such temptation. As for testosterone, it decreases generosity, perhaps one reason why women make more generous offers than men, while oxytocin has the opposite effect.

Should we start pumping oxytocin through the air conditioning system? The precautionary principle counsels us to err on the side of caution. For one thing, if we meddle with hormones like oxytocin, serotonin, or testosterone, the result will never be straightforward. These are Stakhanovite little hormones: they do tireless work in the brain and they're interconnected. So an intervention the effect of which is generally considered positive may produce negative consequences too. Some outcomes may prove not just deleterious but irreversible.

What's more, an alteration that appears beneficial in one context may be harmful in another. A sniff of oxytocin up the nostrils makes people more trusting: society as a whole might function better if we all trusted each other a little more. On the other hand, we wouldn't want the young woman who leaves a club on a Saturday night with a man she's just met to be overly trusting.[7]

There are reasons, therefore, to be wary of the new scientific and technological possibilities. On the whole, evolution has equipped us reasonably well. We don't always trust people, since not everyone is worthy of our trust. But evolution hasn't got it right in every particular. It would surely be better if we were more concerned about the plight of distant strangers. There are well-known studies that show that if we hear about a tragedy that's befallen one particular individual we are more likely to care than if we hear news of one that's befallen thousands. That's not rational. And although we need to weigh the risks of taking action to improve ourselves ethically, enhancement may in certain circumstances be not only acceptable but morally essential.

PART 4

The Trolley and Its Critics

A Streetcar Named Backfire

I don't do trolleys.

THAT WAS A DISMISSIVE COMMENT of an excellent philosopher, approached to discuss trolleyology.[1] "It's symptomatic of a disease in moral philosophy," moaned another.

Some moral philosophers devote their lives to trolley-type dilemmas. Many more cite trolleyology in lectures and seminars and instruct their students to read at least part of the trolley literature. But trolleyology turns the grey matter of other philosophers red. They would like to shunt the trolleys into a remote retirement depot. Philippa Foot is held unwittingly responsible for creating a Frankensteinian monster.

The fear and loathing are worth trying to understand.

It cannot be a suspicion of thought experiments generally. Trolleyology has to be seen within a broader context. Thought experiments and extended metaphors are the meat and potatoes of philosophy—part of the staple diet not just in moral philosophy but in all sub-genres of the discipline. Plato, in *The Republic*, has the famous allegory of the cave: prisoners shackled in a cave look at shadows on the wall that they mistakenly take for actual people. In fact, the shadows are caused by puppeteers manipulating puppets behind them. Plato is making a point about how deeply detached we are from reality. In *Meditations*, the father of modern philosophy René Descartes raises the possibility that an evil demon has fooled us into believing even things about which we feel certain, such as 2+3=5. John Locke has a famous thought experiment in which the soul of a prince—with all the prince's thoughts and memories—is transferred into the body of a cobbler. What makes a person the same person over time is not the body but consciousness, Locke believed. In the eighteenth century, Kant imagines a hypothetical case about a hunted, innocent man who takes refuge in your house. A murderer knocks on the door and demands to know whether his quarry is hiding inside. (Kant claimed it would be wrong, even in these circumstances, to lie.) Wittgenstein tried to demonstrate the absurdity of a private language—a language that (necessarily) only one individual could use—by imagining we each had a matchbox inside that was something we all referred to as a "beetle," but I couldn't look into your box and you couldn't look into mine. In that case, said Wittgenstein, the term beetle could not refer to a particular thing—since we might all have different things in our boxes.[2]

More recently, in the second half of the twentieth century, Robert Nozick asked whether we would plug into an Experience Machine.[3] So ingenious was this hypothetical gadget that we would instantly forget that we were connected to it, and we would be guaranteed pleasurable "experiences" (for example, that we'd won a Nobel Prize or scored the winning goal with a spectacular overhead kick in the World Cup final). None of these experiences would be real, but we would believe they were. Derek Parfit borrowed from science fiction to moot disquieting questions about personal identity: would we be the same person if a tele-transporter made a copy of all the molecules in our bodies and reconstituted them on another planet?[4] And John Searle imagined a Chinese Room. In this room a person is passed notes in Chinese under a door. Although he doesn't speak Chinese, he follows a complex set of instructions from a manual, copies out the response prescribed by this manual, and passes a response back under the door. From outside the room we might assume he understands Chinese, when in fact he can't understand a word. It's a thought experiment designed to suggest that computers will never really think or understand.[5]

So thought experiments have littered philosophical texts through the ages. It seems implausible that they, collectively, are the main target for the trolleyphobes. It's possible that the trolleyphobes have a more specific objection to their use in the moral realm. But even that seems farfetched: notable moral philosophers from all traditions—utilitarian, Aristotelian, Kantian—have deployed thought experiments in argument or illustration.

True, there are doubts about the reliability of our intuitions in the trolley cases (see chapter 10). Our intuitions can be easily manipulated and are influenced by morally irrelevant factors. Some of the trolley problems are so outlandish that it's not clear how we should react to them. Moreover, even those scenarios that do elicit near-universal responses are unusual or artificial, so a case needs to be made for their applicability beyond the seminar room. Cases that are odd may not necessarily be reliable guides to cases that are ordinary.

But the strongest critics of trolleyology want to attack it at a deeper level still. Trolleyology is essentially about what people should do. Should they turn the trolley? Should they push the fat man? But there's a tradition going back to Aristotle which stresses another question. What matters is less about what people do, more about what kind of character they have. Are they brave, cowardly, generous, mean, truthful, dishonest? What virtues and vices do they possess?[6]

The idea that a virtuous person could also be someone who would weigh the costs and benefits of pushing a man to his death is, at least according to Bernard Williams, an incoherent one. In his words, practical thought cannot be "transcendental to experience."[7] In other words, a generous person just is someone who is motivated to act generously, and then does so. It is a sort of nonsense to describe a person as being, say, honest, if that person is prepared to act dishonestly whenever utilitarianism so dictates.

Philippa Foot, the unwitting founder of trolleyology, would not disagree. She and her friends, Elizabeth Anscombe and Iris Murdoch, helped resurrect the tradition of virtue ethics. Murdoch gives an imaginary example, much quoted. A mother-in-law, apparently driven by jealousy and snobbery, has a very low opinion of her daughter-in-law. She regards her daughter-in-law as rude, juvenile, lacking in dignity and refinement. But then, after careful reflection, she comes to see these characteristics differently: the daughter-in-law is no longer undignified but spontaneous.

Naturally, as a result of this change of perspective, the mother-in-law acts differently toward her daughter-in-law. But the action is, as it were, secondary to the seeing: and it's in the seeing correctly that the hard moral work is done. In his book *Nicomachean Ethics*, Aristotle distinguishes between types of wisdom. There is theoretical wisdom, but there is also *phronēsis*, which is usually translated as "practical wisdom." According to neo-Aristotelians, a person with *phronēsis* is able to sense what is the right thing to do.

Very Particular(ist)

The instincts of the trolleyologist are not dissimilar to those of the scientist, in the following regard at least. The trolleyologist wants to determine what moral distinctions are relevant, and to prod and poke, weigh, compare, and contrast our intuitions. The trolleyologist wants to make use of "clean" cases to aid our moral navigation in a messy world. But this is not how the Aristotelian conceptualizes the moral realm. The person with *phronēsis* is not in possession of any kind of moral algorithm, and has not mastered morality through any abstract investigation of it. This person has, instead, in a nice phrase used by one philosopher, "situational appreciation."[8]

The extreme end of this line of thinking is the moral particularist.[9] According to the particularist there are no correct moral maxims or principles, be they consequentialist (e.g., "always maximize happiness"), or deontologist (e.g., "never lie"). Each case is unique. There will be relevant moral considerations of course: whether an action involves lying, perhaps, or whether it causes suffering. Sometimes the moral particularist might want to cite the Doctrine of Double Effect. But there are no hard-and-fast rules: at best there are rules of thumb. Ethical thinking cannot be systematized in the way the trolleyologist would like it to be. The trolleyologist's project is thus, inevitably, doomed from the start.

These are the big objections to trolleyology. One suspects, too, the existence of a more trivial and unjust one. There's a sense that the trolley problem is, damn it, just too much fun, and fun is a quality incompatible with intellectual weightiness. It feels a bit like a brain teaser that might be published by a newspaper on its puzzle page next to the sudoku. Peter Singer is one philosopher wary of reducing "philosophy . . . to the level of solving the chess puzzle."[10] Though he used to love chess puzzles, "there are things that are more important."[11]

This would seem a particularly harsh indictment if it were leveled at a philosopher like Kamm, whose entire philosophical life has been devoted to trolley-like conundrums. Whatever it is that motivates Professor Kamm, it's not a sense of fun. "I am always surprised when people say, 'Oh, that was a nice discussion. That was fun.' I think, 'Fun?' *Fun?* This is a serious matter. . . . If we had worked on a NASA rocket and it launched well, we wouldn't say, 'Well, that was fun!' . . . It was awe-inspiring—that would be the right way of putting it!"[12]

In the end, trolleyologists and trolleyphobes have to agree to differ. Dismissing this entire approach to ethics as worthless means jettisoning scores of books and hundreds of articles by dozens of serious thinkers. Derek Parfit's book *Reasons and Persons* is hailed as one of the seminal works in moral philosophy of the past few decades—but, though the work doesn't itself discuss trolley problems, it exemplifies the trolley method of philosophy. It's rich in imaginative thought experiments and it derives principles from testing intuitions in myriad fantasy scenarios. This is just one of numerous books in this "genre." If trolleyology is misguided, then so are many publications based on trolleyesque argumentation. A rejection of the entire methodology would imply that many philosophers have been wasting their time. ("It wouldn't be the first time," said one eminent former Oxford professor, sotto voce.) Should that not give us pause?

The Terminal

Truth is incontrovertible, malice may attack it, ignorance may deride it, but in the end, there it is.

—Winston Churchill

AFTER HURRICANE KATRINA flattened parts of New Orleans in 2005, one member of the National Guard was quoted as saying: " I would be looking at a family of two on one roof and maybe a family of six on another roof, and I would have to make a decision who to rescue."[1]

Residents of Bangkok would later have some special empathy with this predicament. In 2011, the Chao Phraya, a river that meanders through the Thai capital, Bangkok, became dangerously swollen, reaching more than three meters above its normal level. Floods that summer had already cost hundreds of lives. In an attempt to save the city center, where many people lived, where the tourists came to spend their money, and where major businesses were based, the authorities had built a ring of dikes and sandbags, fifteen kilometers long. But, while this left the center reasonably dry, it caused a buildup of water outside the protected zone. Enraged and desperate residents in the north, west, and east of the city demanded that holes be cut in the ring to allow the rising and stagnating water to flow through. Police positioned hundreds of officers around the protected zone to prevent the floodwalls being sabotaged.

Such real-life dilemmas would appear familiar to trolleyologists. The trolley industry is currently in robust health. It has been boosted by developments in psychology and neuroethics and by the nascent but burgeoning field of experimental ethics. Trolley-type problems pop up in real life, while trolley thought experiments continue to crop up in academic philosophy papers.

But, like most industries, it will inevitably peak at some stage and then decline. Not before time, some philosophers might add. Certainly it's difficult to imagine how new variations on the trolley theme could provide much additional illumination. The complexity of existing scenarios has already been stretched to the limits of our credulity and imagination — limits beyond which intuitions become fuzzy and faint.

The aim of trolleyology is to provide a principle or principles that make sense of our powerful reactions and that can reveal something to us about the nature of morality. It's been a protracted philosophical detective story: different scenarios have provided different pieces of evidence to support different conclusions.

But it remains possible that the founders of trolleyology, Foot and Thomson, inadvertently pushed their trolleys down the wrong path.

In Agatha Christie's mystery novel, *Death on the Nile*, the reader is led to believe that the murderer can't be the obvious candidate (for she, apparently, has a cast-iron alibi). Later, Hercule Poirot, the little Belgian detective with the curly mustache, realizes that he has been bamboozled: the obvious candidate (with the support of an accomplice) was guilty all along.

Foot and Thomson both rejected an appeal to the Doctrine

of Double Effect. Yet this doctrine, first identified almost a millennium ago by Thomas Aquinas, has powerful intuitive resonance. At its heart is the difference between intending and merely foreseeing—in Spur we foresee but do not intend a death, in Fat Man we do. This is not a distinction that carries any weight with utilitarians—for in both Spur and Fat Man, the consequences of saving the five are the same: one man will die. But most non-utilitarians regard it as obvious that the nature of an intention is relevant in the judgment of an action.

If the distinction between intention and foreseeing holds the solution to our moral conundrum—as it seems to me that it does—then Thomson's Loop dilemma was a giant red herring. How could a few extra meters of track make any moral difference, she asked? Her answer was that it couldn't. And that set philosophers fishing for an alternative principle. But those few extra meters might make a moral difference—after all, in Loop it looks as if we intend to kill the one man on the track. As we've seen from the experimental work, if Loop is shown before exposure to Spur, rather than after, subjects are much more likely to judge that turning the trolley is impermissible. Thompson's intuition ceases to command undivided support.

The Doctrine of Double Effect offers an explanation for the moral difference between Spur and Fat Man. It is an explanation with many virtues: it is simple and economic, it doesn't seem arbitrary, and it has intuitive appeal across a broad range of cases. It is the reason why the fat man would be safe from me at least.

End of the Line

What happened to the characters featured in this book? What was their fate?

Grover Cleveland's chief trolley problem, George Pullman, lived only three more years after the strike of 1894. A national commission set up to examine the strike's causes concluded that Pullman's company town was un-American. Such was the loathing for Pullman that even he couldn't delude himself about it—and he made arrangements to ensure his body was not desecrated after his death. He was buried in a lead-lined coffin within a steel-and-concrete vault. The Pullman company went into rapid decline. President Cleveland never fully recovered from the strike either, failing to win the renomination at the 1896 Democratic National Convention.

• • •

Cleveland's daughter, Esther, met her future husband on a trip to London. Their daughter Pip gave up her Oxford post shortly after her trolley article was published. She took various visiting professorships in the United States, until she became a full professor of philosophy at UCLA. But she continued to spend a lot of time in Oxford and eventually retired there. She died in 2010 on her ninetieth birthday. All the newspaper obituaries about her mention the trolley problem.

• • •

Despite the furious denunciation by Foot's friend, Elizabeth Anscombe, Harry Truman was awarded his Oxford honorary doctorate. He rather dismissively called it his "floppy hat" degree, referring to the black velvet headgear that honorands are required to wear. Before the ceremony, he gave a press conference denying any knowledge of the furor that Anscombe had created. "The English are very polite. They kept it from me."[2] And he reiterated that he had no regrets about dropping the atomic bomb. "If I had to do it again, I would do it all over again."[3] He entered the Sheldonian at midday on June 20, 1956 to "God Save the Queen," and wearing his vivid scarlet robe, took his place on an eighteenth-century mahogany hall chair, decorated with elaborate coats of arms, and reserved for just this occasion. All around the theater applause broke out, redoubling as Truman stood and bowed.

• • •

Anscombe herself stayed away from the ceremony—to no one's surprise. She was quoted by a newspaper as saying she would spend the day working as usual. But the arguments she deployed in her tirade against Truman were influential in not only shifting Catholic policy on war (the Catholic Church in Rome had remained almost entirely silent about the aerial bombardments of German cities in World War II), but, more generally, in having "Just War" theory accepted within the military and beyond.

Her academic career blossomed. She became Professor of Philosophy at Cambridge University in 1970. This had been her mentor Ludwig Wittgenstein's post. She remained a staunch Roman Catholic and was twice arrested protesting outside an abortion clinic. She retired in 1986, died in 2001, and was buried in a grave next to Wittgenstein. She and Pip Foot had drifted apart: Anscombe admitted to always feeling terrible that she couldn't convince Foot that there was a God.

• • •

Iris Murdoch died in 1999, having spent the last few years of her life suffering from Alzheimer's disease, a period that was documented in a book by her husband John Bailey, and later turned into a successful movie, *Iris*. It is said that when Murdoch became ill, Philippa Foot was one of the very few people with whom she could be left alone without becoming agitated.[4] Murdoch will be remembered more for her novels than for her philosophy. She once said that she had loved Foot, "more than I ever thought I could love any woman,"[5] and Foot appears in various guises in Murdoch's novels. But when Murdoch died, Foot admitted that there was something about Murdoch she'd always found unfathomable. "We lived together for two years in the war, and she and I were the closest of friends to the end. Yet I never felt I altogether knew her. . . ."[6]

• • •

The cannibal case of *Regina v. Dudley and Stephens*, which had caused such a sensation in the late Victorian era, was soon forgotten in Britain. Dudley and Stephens, prisoners 5331 and 5332, returned to jail to serve their shortened sentence. On his release, Dudley emigrated to Australia: he died in 1900 at just forty-six years old after contracting bubonic plague. Stephens returned to a seafaring life: it's thought he became depressed and took to drink. He died in poverty. Brooks salvaged the story from complete obscurity by appearing on several occasions in "amusement shows," the nineteenth-century version of the celebrity circuit.

• • •

After the operation on their conjoined twins, in which Mary died but Jodie survived, Rina Attard and her husband moved back to the island of Goma, off Malta, and live with Jodie quietly there still. They are reported to be pleased in retrospect that the legal judgment went against them.

• • •

As for the quasi ticking-bomb–like scenario in Germany, Magnus Gäfgen was convicted and sentenced to life imprisonment for murder and kidnapping with extortion. But the legal ramifications rumbled on for years. The case eventually went to the European Court of Human Rights, where Germany was convicted of violating the prohibition against torture and inhuman and degrading treatment. Gäfgen also sued the state of Hesse, demanding compensation for the trauma he experienced from the torture threat. In 2011, a German court awarded him 3,000 Euros in damages. The police officer behind the torture threat, Wolfgang Daschner, had already been fined and transferred to other duties. Meanwhile, Gäfgen had completed his law degree, though his plan to establish "a Gäfgen Foundation" to help child victims of crime was withdrawn—the authorities said they would never permit it to be registered.

• • •

For the past half century, trolleyology has provided a vehicle to contest fundamental issues in ethics—vital questions about how we should treat others and live our lives. When Philippa Foot introduced the trolley problem it was to intervene in the debate over abortion. Nowadays, a trolley-like challenge is more likely to arise in deliberations about the legitimacy of types of conduct in warfare. Churchill's dilemma—about whether to attempt to redirect rockets to less populous areas—

continues to be reincarnated in a variety of other forms too. The Fat Man quandary highlights the stark clash between deontological and utilitarian ethics. Most people do not have utilitarian instincts (as utilitarians themselves acknowledge). They believe that Winston Churchill would have been wrong to use citizens as a human shield, even if his objective was to save the lives of others. He would have been equally wrong to force or inveigle people into the path of a Nazi threat, even if in order to save lives. But, on balance, he was surely right to support the deception plot to redirect the doodlebugs toward south London.

Why the difference? Philosophers still can't agree. But whatever the answer, the strange situation of the fat man on the footbridge must hold the key. I wouldn't kill the fat man. Would you?

Appendix

Ten Trolleys: A Rerun

Figure 1. *Spur.* You're standing by the side of a track when you see a run-away train hurtling toward you: clearly the brakes have failed. Ahead are five people, tied to the track. If you do nothing, the five will be run over and killed. Luckily you are next to a signal switch: turning this switch will send the out-of-control train down a side track, a spur, just ahead of you. Alas, there's a snag: on the spur you spot one person tied to the track: changing direction will inevitably result in this person being killed. What should you do?

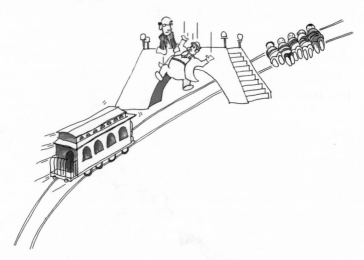

Figure 2. *Fat Man.* You're on a footbridge overlooking the railway track. You see the trolley hurtling along the track and, ahead of it, five people tied to the rails. Can these five be saved? Again, the moral philosopher has cunningly arranged matters so that they can be. There's a very fat man leaning over the railing watching the trolley. If you were to push him over the footbridge, he would tumble down and smash on to the track below. He's so obese that his bulk would bring the trolley to a shuddering halt. Sadly, the process would kill the fat man. But it would save the other five. Should you push the fat man?

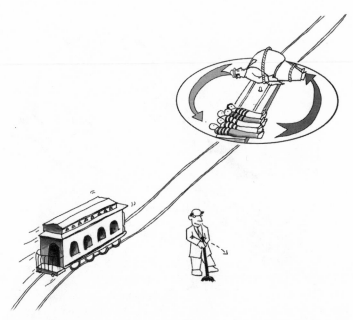

Figure 3. *Lazy Susan.* In Lazy Susan you can save the five by twisting the revolving plate 180 degrees—this will have the unfortunate consequence of placing one man directly in the path of the train. Should you rotate the Lazy Susan?

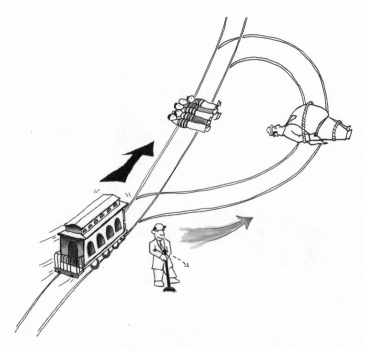

Figure 4. *Loop.* The trolley is heading toward five men who, as it happens, are all skinny. If the trolley were to collide into them they would die, but their combined bulk would stop the train. You could instead turn the trolley onto a loop. One fat man is tied onto the loop. His weight alone will stop the trolley, preventing it from continuing around the loop and killing the five. Should you turn the trolley down the loop?

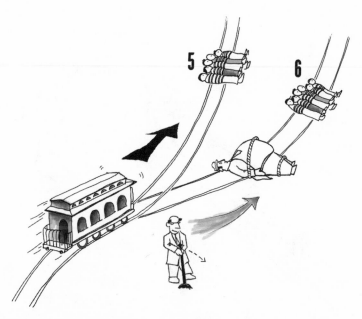

Figure 5. *Six Behind One.* You are standing on the side of the track. A runaway trolley is hurtling toward you. Ahead are five people, tied to the track. If you do nothing, the five will be run over and killed. Luckily you are next to a signal switch: turning this switch will send the out-of-control trolley down a side track, a spur, just ahead of you. On the spur you see one person tied to the track: changing direction will inevitably result in this person being killed. Behind the one person are six people, also tied to the track. The one person, if hit, will stop the trolley. What should you do?

This example is from Otsuka 2008.

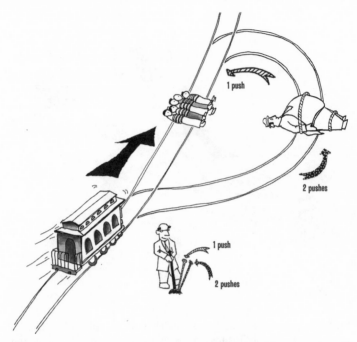

Figure 6. *Extra Push.* The trolley is heading toward the five men who will die if you do nothing. You can turn the trolley onto a loop away from the five men. On this loop is a single man. But the trolley is traveling at such a pace that it would jump over the one man on the side track unless given an extra push. If it jumped over this man, it would loop back and kill the five. The only way to guarantee that it crashes into the man is to give it an extra push. Should you turn the trolley, and should you also give it the extra push?

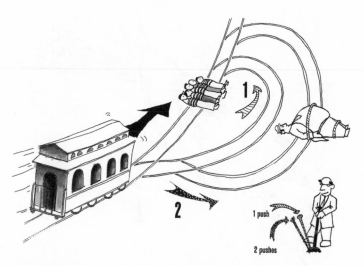

Figure 7. *Two Loop.* The trolley is heading toward five men who will die if you do nothing. You can redirect the trolley onto an empty loop. If you took no further action, the trolley would rattle around this loop and kill the five. However, you could redirect the trolley a second time down a second loop that does have one person on it. This would kill the person on the track but save the five lives. Should you redirect the trolley, not once, but twice?

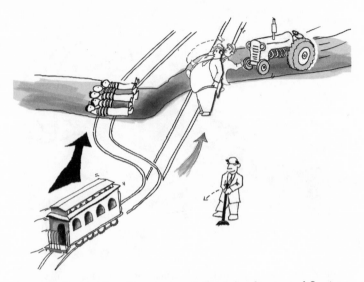

Figure 8. *Tractor Man*. The runaway trolley is heading toward five innocents. The trolley is not the only thing they're threatened by. They are also about to be flattened by another, independent, threat. Rampaging in their direction is an out-of-control tractor. To redirect the trolley would be pointless if the five were in any case to be hit by the tractor. But if you turn the trolley away from them, it will gently hit and push, without hurting, another person into the path of the tractor. His being hit by the tractor would stop that vehicle but also kill him. Should you redirect the trolley?

Figure 9. *The Tumble Case.* The runaway trolley is heading toward five people. You cannot redirect the trolley, but you can move the five. But if you did that, the five would tumble down a mountain and, although they themselves would be unharmed, their body weight would kill an innocent person below. Should you move the five?

Figure 10. *The Trap Door.* The runaway trolley is heading toward five people. You are standing by the side of the track. The only way to stop the trolley killing the five is to pull a lever which opens a trap door on which a fat man happens to be standing. The fat man would plummet to the ground and die, but his body would stop the trolley. Should you open the trap door?

Notes

Chapter 1: Churchill's Dilemma

1. Lehmann 1968, 199.
2. Waugh 1999, 615.
3. An ex con named Eddie Chapman.
4. Spanish-born Juan Pujol Garcia, who convinced the Nazis that he ran a network of informers—all of whom were fictitious.
5. Jones 1978, 423.
6. In fact, although no more V1s would reach Britain, the Nazis were about to unleash a new long-range weapon, the V2.

Chapter 2: Spur of the Moment

1. Foot 2002.
2. There's no evidence that when Philippa Foot came up with her train conundrum she knew about the World War II parallel.
3. The term was first coined by Kwame Anthony Appiah—an act of denomination of which he's proud.
4. TED talk: interviewer was Chris Anderson; see http://www.ted.com/talks/gordon_brown_on_global_ethic_vs_national_interest.html. TED, which stands for Technology, Entertainment, Design, is an organization dedicated to the spread of worthwhile ideas.
5. Many philosophers believe that there are special deontological constraints that apply to killing but not to unintentionally allowing people to die. My thanks to Jeff McMahan for highlighting this point. Of course, in deciding which drug to fund, a drug's impact on the quality as well as the length of life will be relevant.
6. See Appiah 2008, 91.

Chapter 3: The Founding Mothers

1. Ayer returned to Oxford to spread the gospel of logical positivism. Shortly afterward—a wretched irony this—the Vienna Circle itself fell victim to the Nazi jackboot, its members scattering to Chicago, Princeton, Oxford, and elsewhere.

2. Magee 1978, 131.

3. Also known as "emotivism." Emotivism is not quite the same as subjectivism, another -ism that Foot rejected. Subjectivism says that when I say "murder is wrong," I *state* my disapproval, whereas emotivism claims that in that sentence I merely express it. It is an expression, not an assertion.

4. The impact of ordinary language philosophy was still very much felt when I studied undergraduate and postgraduate philosophy in Oxford in the 1980s. I recall having a particularly spirited discussion with one of my tutors about the distinction between a cup and a mug.

5. Author interview with Lesley Brown.

6. Quoted in *The Financial Times*, *The Daily Telegraph*, and *The Independent* in obituaries of Philippa Foot published in October 2010.

7. Midgely 2005, 52.

8. Conradi 2001, 185.

9. Letter to author from Daphne Stroud.

10. Teichmann 2008, 3.

11. Author interview with Lesley Brown.

12. M.R.D. Foot 2008, 83.

13. Murdoch 2010, 254–55.

14. M.R.D. Foot 2008, 78.

15. Murdoch 2010, 254.

16. Conradi 2001, 223.

17. M.R.D. Foot 2008, 130.

18. Although Crisp (2012) argues that virtue ethics is an offshoot of deontology.

19. According to Michael Dummett in an address at Philippa Foot's memorial on March 19, 2011.

20. Interview with author.

21. Foot 2001, 1.

22. Wittgenstein 1953, 103.

23. According to Michael Dummett in an address at Philippa Foot's memorial.

24. Anscombe 1956, 5.

25. A.F.L. Beeston, quoted in Glover 2001, 106. Beeston claims that the full house was entirely unrelated to Truman. Instead the congregation had shown up because of irritation at a plan to cut down on the use of the Greek New Testament in the theology degree. He says that "the speech elicited only the complete silence and impassivity of those present . . . not the slightest sign of approval or disapproval, not a murmur, not

a rustle, not a change of countenance, but only utter imperturbability." But the claim of "utter imperturbability" seems implausible and is at odds with the media coverage.

26. *Oxford Mail*, May 1, 1956.

27. Anscombe told Tony Kenny that three people had supported her.

28. Interview with author.

29. Voorhoeve 2009, 93.

Chapter 4: The Seventh Son of Count Landulf

1. What is it with philosophers and pokers? For more poker action, see Edmonds and Eidinow 2001.

2. Some scholars say there is an echo of the DDE in the biblical principle of the apostle Paul in Romans 3:8. One ought not "do evil that good may come."

3. Interview with author.

4. Voorhoeve 2009, 87.

5. Foot, *Virtues and Vices*, 2002, 20. Although most of the founding fathers of trolleyology were in fact women, the language they use in their papers reflects the gender bias of its time.

6. Discussed in Wiggins 2006, 250–51.

7. Interview with author.

8. Scanlon 2008, 18.

9. Foot, *Virtues and Vices*, 2002, 21.

10. This is an adapted version from Foot, *Virtues and Vices*, 2002, 24–25.

11. More about this in chapter 11.

Chapter 5: Fat Man, Loop, and Lazy Susan

1. Both are reproduced in Thomson 1986. They originally appeared as "Killing, Letting Die and the Trolley Problem" (*The Monist*, 1976) and "The Trolley Problem" (*Yale Law Journal* 94, 1985).

2. Jeff McMahan pointed out to me that if the fat man throws himself off the bridge he would be using himself—in Kantian language—as a mere means to an end. A problem with Kant's view is that it seems to condemn self-sacrifice; yet no philosopher—Kantian or otherwise—wants to say that it is impermissible to kill oneself intentionally for the sake of others.

3. Also in Thomson 1986.

4. Thomson 1986, 108.

5. Thomson 1986, 108.

6. Frances Kamm.

7. Kamm 2007, 24.

8. Gottfried Leibniz (1646–1716) was a German mathematician and philosopher. The French enlightenment writer Voltaire uses his character Pangloss, in the novella *Candide*, to draw a thinly disguised parody of Leibniz.

9. Thomson 1986, 102.

10. It's worth noting that Thomson has addressed the trolley problem several times, and given four quite distinct responses to it. She eventually came to believe that it was wrong to turn the trolley in Loop and, what's more, it was even wrong to turn the trolley in Spur.

Chapter 6: Ticking Clocks and the Sage of Königsberg

1. Quoted in *International Herald Tribune*, April 11, 2003.

2. Quoted in *Washington Post*, March 8, 2003.

3. Quoted in *New York Times*, April 11, 2003.

4. Quoted on *Deutsche Welle* web page, February 24, 2003.

5. Naturally this required an ignorant or at least partial misreading of Kant. The Categorical Imperative has a golden rule formulation: only act in a certain way if you could will it that all people act in this way. Eichmann believed that the Categorical Imperative only required a person's actions to coincide with a general law—regardless of the moral content of this law.

6. In "Morality, Action and Outcome" in Honderich 1985, 36.

7. Dershowitz 2002, 141.

8. It's worth pointing out that at least one well-known antiutilitarian, Bernard Williams, describes this defense of absolutism as "a cop out." See "Utilitarianism and Moral Self-indulgence" in Williams 1981, 43.

9. This is Jeff McMahan's position. I'm grateful to Professor McMahan for his extremely helpful comments on this chapter.

10. Rai Gaita interview for Philosophy Bites: www.philosophybites.com.

11. Dostoyevsky 1991, 245–46.

12. In "Killing and Letting Die" in Foot, *Moral Dilemmas*, 2002, 79.

13. This example is from James Rachels, "Active and Passive Euthanasia," 115, reprinted in Steinbock and Norcross 1994.

14. Shelly Kagan makes a similar point in *The Additive Fallacy* (1988).

15. In the BBC World Service documentary, *Would You Kill The Big Guy* (May 2010).

16. Kamm 2007, 95.

17. Although Kamm draws this clever distinction, she herself believes that in virtually all cases the intention with which an act is done is irrelevant to whether or not the action is permissible. She believes that the relevant facts have to do not with mental states but with causal relations. The key question for her is whether killing the one is a causally necessary means to saving the five.

Chapter 7: Paving the Road to Hell

1. Cleveland 1904, 109.

2. Papke 1999, 30.

3. Cleveland: Proclamation 366: July 8, 1894.

4. Anscombe 1957.

5. Anscombe 2003, 32.

6. From p. xlvi of report, available online at http://archive.org/stream/reportonchicago00wriggoog#page/n6/mode/2up.

7. Foot, *Virtues and Vices* 2002, 21. See also Bennett 1995, 210–11. Bennett imagines a bomber during a war who wants to lower morale among enemy civilians and so targets and kills some of them in a raid. However, he claims he doesn't intend to kill them, he only intends that they should appear dead for a year or two until the war is over!

8. Nagel 1986, 181.

9. Nagel 1986, 182. Nagel believes that if you are "guided by evil" you will adjust your response to changed circumstances. But even if you adjust your response to changes in a trolley scenario, that doesn't imply that you are "guided by evil" in a deeper sense. Thus, if the five were to escape, you wouldn't want to still kill the fat man. Nonetheless, our understanding of intentionality is deepened by Nagel's insight that we reflect on what we would do in alternative situations.

10. Kamm 2007, 97–99.

11. Kamm 2007, 97. Strangely, Kamm wants to draw a distinction between Extra Push and Two Loop. She thinks it's wrong to give the trolley

an Extra Push, but it is perfectly legitimate to redirect the trolley again in Two Loop. It seems to me that they are morally on a par, and that giving the trolley an extra push or redirecting the trolley onto the second loop both make the intention to hit the one unambiguous.

Chapter 8: Morals by Numbers

1. Mill 1980, 44.
2. Russell 1977, 85.
3. Brougham 1838, 287.
4. King 1976, 2.
5. Bentham 1970, footnote on p. 283.
6. William Empson, *Cobbett's Political Register*, December 12, 1818.
7. Dinwiddy 1984, 23.
8. Bassett and Spenser 1929, 146.
9. Bowring, *The Works*, vol. 10, 57, 63; also see vol. 2, 493–94.
10. Bowring, *The Works*, vol. 2, 497.
11. Bowring, *The Works*, vol. 2, 501.
12. Quoted by Conway 1989, 87.
13. *The Principles of International Law: Essay 4* (A Plan for an Universal and Perpetual Peace).
14. Though it's worth noting that the source for this is Mill's *Autobiography*, which might peddle some family myths.
15. Mill 1980, 44.
16. Mill 1992, 37.
17. Bentham 1830, 206.
18. Mill, 2002, chapter II, paragraph 6.
19. Mill 1992, 60.
20. Mill is sometimes described as a "rule utilitarian," though this is a contentious label for him. A rule utilitarian believes that an action is right insofar as it conforms to a rule that leads to the greatest good. Rule utilitarians believe that even if, on a particular occasion, it would be better to break the rule in order to maximize happiness or well-being, nonetheless, one should abide by the rule.
21. Sidgwick 1962, 490.
22. Williams 1985, 108. With this phrase Williams was drawing attention to what he called "the important colonialist connections of utilitarianism."
23. Sidgwick 1962, 490.

24. Ibid., 489.

25. See, e.g., Hare 1981. He calls his two levels of thinking the intuitive and the critical.

26. It should be said that there are a few consequentialists—Brad Hooker is the best known—who believe that what we should do is identify the rules that maximize happiness or well-being and stick to these rules even if on certain occasions we could increase happiness or well-being by violating these rules.

27. Both scenarios are in Smart and Williams 1973, 97–100.

28. A phrase used by Henry Sidgwick: Sidgwick 1962, 382.

Chapter 9: Out of the Armchair

1. Barry Smith, interview on BBC *Analysis* program, June 28, 2009.

2. And note that David Hume's seminal work, *A Treatise of Human Nature,* had, as its subtitle *Being an Attempt to Introduce the Experimental Methods of Reasoning into Moral Subjects.*

3. Joshua Knobe, interview on *Philosophy Bites* (www.philosophy-bites.com).

4. Thomson 1986, 107 (my italics).

5. Email correspondence with author.

6. See Weinberg et al., 2001. This is not a result that others have managed to replicate.

7. See Knobe and Nichols 2008, chap. 6, "Moral Responsibility and Determinism."

8. Hugh Mellor, quoted in "Philosophy's Great Experiment," *Prospect Magazine,* March 2009.

Chapter 10: It Just *Feels* Wrong

1. Some utilitarians are of the view that we should give little or no weight to our intuitions. But the majority of moral philosophers place great weight on them. In an article entitled "The Wisdom of Repugnance" the former chairman of the President's Council on Bioethics, Leon Kass, says he is "repelled" by the prospect of cloning humans. He claims that "we intuit and feel, immediately and without argument, the violation of things that we rightfully hold dear."

2. Kamm 2007, 137.

3. Although a couple of studies cast doubt on the idea of philosopher as "expert." See, for example, Cushman et al. 2012.

4. Email to author.

5. Unger 1996, chapter 4.

6. Liao et al. 2011, 661–71. In an email, Jeff McMahan told me that he got similar results when testing his students for ordering effects.

Chapter 11: Dudley's Choice and the Moral Instinct

1. "Usually," because there are moral relativists who deny that morality is universal.

2. In such a phrase the convention is that opinion (terrifying) comes before dimension (large), which comes before color (black). But "the large, terrifying, black trolley" might strike people as acceptable too.

3. Mikhail 2011, 101. There had already been some classic works on the development of morality in children: see, for example, Piaget 1977.

4. Hauser 2006, 34. Hauser was later disgraced, after reports surfaced of research malpractice: but there has been no suggestion that there was anything untoward about the published results in this field of study.

5. For these and other manipulations of the trolley examples, see Mikhail 2011, 106–9.

6. Powers 1987, 23.

7. Simpson 1994, 61.

8. Ibid., 62.

9. Ibid., 69.

10. Hanson 2000, 272.

11. See Simpson 1988

12. Royal Courts of Justice, September 22, 2000, Case No. B1/2000/2969.

13. Hauser 2006, 126.

14. I've put quotation marks around words like "autonomy" and "agent" because philosophers disagree about whether machines could ever really be autonomous or ever really be moral agents.

Chapter 12: The Irrational Animal

1. The experiment, devised shortly after the Nazi war criminal Adolf Eichmann's trial in Jerusalem, was designed to test how badly people

would behave if under instruction from authority figures. Subjects were told that people on the other side of the wall were to learn words. The subjects were ordered to administer electric shocks to the learners if these learners made mistakes in questions about the words. In fact, the learners were actors. The subjects could hear (fake) screams and the learners banging on the wall in (apparent) desperation.

2. Princeton Theological Seminary is an educational establishment that stresses the virtue of charity and that itself possesses staggering wealth. As of 2011, it had an endowment per student of nearly $1.7 million.

3. Darley and Batson 1973, 100–108.

4. Danziger et al. 2011.

5. *Philosophy Bites* interview, "Experiments in Ethics": www.philoso-phybites.com.

6. And choosing the nonutilitarian option—death of the five—was also linked to emotional arousal. See Navarrete et al. 2012.

7. See Valdesolo et al. 2006.

8. Uhlmann et al. 2009.

9. In Thomson 1990, 292, she writes that it would "be permissible to kill one chicken to save five chickens." McMahan 2002, chapter 3, also examines whether deontological constraints apply to animals.

10. Hume 1975, 415.

11. Haidt 2001.

12. Some philosophers don't accept Haidt's analysis of such cases. If people run out of reasons for why they believe incest is wrong, that doesn't imply that they are "dumbfounded." "Incest is wrong" may simply be a foundational principle—a principle that is self-evident, that is, requires no further justification.

13. See Wheatley and Haidt 2005.

Chapter 13: Wrestling with Neurons

1. Damasio has an excellent account of the Phineas Gage story. The historical facts about Gage have been disputed: some say that his behavior changed significantly only later in his life.

2. Interview for the BBC *Analysis* program, broadcast June 28, 2009.

3. Interview with J. Greene for the BBC World Service series *Would you Kill the Big Guy?*

4. Suter 2011, 454–58.

5. Interview with J. Greene for the BBC World Service series *Would you Kill the Big Guy?*

6. Figures from the New America Foundation.

7. Singer 2009, 59.

8. See, for example, Small and Loewenstein 2003.

9. See chapter 8.

10. There are several studies in this area. See, for example, Shepher 1971.

11. A key debate is whether it is useful to draw a distinction between actions that are responsive to reasons and those that are not. For example, an addict is not responsive to rational considerations—so addicts, in one version of compatibilism, do not have free will. But if a person responds to rational reasons, he or she, on this account, acts freely. Thus, if I adore brussels sprouts, I might choose them if they're available on the restaurant menu. But were I to read in a medical journal that brussels sprouts are carcinogenic, then I would avoid them. That shows that my decision to eat or not eat brussels sprouts is "reasons-responsive" and, therefore—according to this version of compatibilism—free.

12. He gives this explanation, for example, in the BBC World Service Series *The Mysteries of the Brain.*

13. Kahneman's *Thinking, Fast and Slow* (2012).

14. This point is well made in a *Philosophy Bites* interview with Neil Levy, at www.philosophybites.com.

15. Singer 2005.

16. See Amit 2012.

17. Suter and Hertwig 2011.

18. E.g., Koenigs et al. 2007.

19. It may not be that they have stronger utilitarian tendencies, but rather weaker deontological ones. Thus, Joshua Greene believes that psychopaths are not best described as more utilitarian: rather, they simply have reduced emotional responses to causing harm. "What they really are is un-deontological" (email to author). Nonetheless, the upshot is that utilitarian considerations are the ones that do the work in reaching contentious judgments—such as that the right thing to do is push the fat man.

20. See Lucas and Sheeran 2006.

21. Though, as described in chapter 12, some psychologists have done their best to replicate real life with 3-D experiments.

22. For the most sustained attack on the new neuroscience, see Tallis 2011.

23. It should be pointed out that there are some philosophers who believe the brain and the mind *are* indeed one and the same thing.

24. Eagleman 2011.

Chapter 14: Bionic Trolley

1. See Terbeck 2012.

2. A 2012 paper (see Terbeck under review) suggests, counterintuitively, that propranolol makes it more likely that people will judge killing the fat man as unacceptable: since propranolol dampens emotion and fear, one might have predicted the opposite effect.

3. See Wright et al. 2012 for research findings on thirst and the ultimatum game.

4. However, primate behavior provides a mixed picture. They haven't tried the Ultimatum Game with capuchin monkeys, but if one monkey receives a piece of cucumber in exchange for a task and observes another monkey receiving a more appetizing grape for the same task, he or she will become extremely angry—and perhaps even reject the cucumber altogether, throwing it away in disgust.

5. Smith 1976, book I, chapter 2, 26–27.

6. Smith 2002, part 1, section I, chapters 1, 11.

7. As an indication of how complex the effect of even an apparently cuddly molecule like oxytocin, see De Dreu et al. 2011. This paper shows oxytocin increases people's biases against an out-group, a bias against a group (say an ethnic group) that isn't one's own.

Chapter 15: A Streetcar Named Backfire

1. Sorry, he (or she) shall remain anonymous.

2. Wittgenstein 1953, 293.

3. Nozick 1974, 42–45.

4. See Parfit 1984, part 3.

5. Searle 1980, 417.

6. Of course, character is not distinct from action. Character, in Aristotle's view, is about dispositions to act. How would a brave man act, or a wise man act? But character also involves feeling. A brave man acts with a certain sentiment.

7. Williams (1981), in an essay entitled "Utilitarianism and moral self-indulgence," 51.

8. See Wiggins, "Deliberation and Practical Reason," in Rorty 1980, 233.

9. A position formulated and best set out by Dancy. See Dancy 1993. The particularist position is problematic in important ways—for example, if we accept particularism, it's not clear how we can adjudicate between different judgments about what is morally appropriate in any particular situation.

10. See Singer interview in Edmonds and Warburton 2010, 26.

11. Ibid.

12. Voorhooeve 2009, 35.

Chapter 16: The Terminal

1. Quoted in Hauser 2006, 35.

2. Quoted in *Oxford Mail*, June 18, 1956.

3. Ibid.

4. A point made by Anne Rowe, of the Centre for Iris Murdoch Studies, and quoted in *The Guardian*, August 31, 2012.

5. Conradi 2001, 220.

6. Warnock 2000, 52, quoting Foot's obituary of Murdoch in *Oxford Today*, Trinity Term 1999.

Bibliography

A note on the bibliography. There are numerous articles and books linked, directly or indirectly, to my topic. Here I list only those articles and books to which I've referred or from which I've quoted, or that have been important in some other way in the writing of this book.

Amit, Elinor, and J. Greene. "You See, the Ends Don't Justify the Means." *Psychological Science*; published online June 28, 2012.

Anscombe, G.E.M. *Mr Truman's Degree* (Oxford: Oxonian Press, 1956).

Anscombe, G.E.M. *Intention* (Oxford: Blackwell, 1957).

Anscombe, G.E.M. *An Introduction to Wittgenstein's* Tractatus (London: Hutchinson, 1971).

Anscombe, G.E.M. *Contraception and Chastity* (London: Catholic Truth Society, 2003 [1975]).

Anscombe, G.E.M. *Human Life, Action and Ethics*, ed. M. Geach and L. Gormally (Exeter: Imprint Academic, 2005).

Appiah, Anthony. *Experiments in Ethics* (Cambridge, MA: Harvard University Press, 2008).

Bassett, J., and J. Spenser, eds. *Correspondence of Andrew Jackson* Vol. 4 (Washington, DC, 1929).

Bennett, Jonathan. *The Act Itself* (Oxford: Clarendon Press, 1995).

Bentham, Jeremy. *The Rationale of Reward* (London: Robert Heward, 1830).

Bentham, Jeremy. *An Introduction to the Principles of Morals and Legislation* (Oxford: Clarendon Press, 1970 [1789]).

Bowring, John, ed. *The Works of Jeremy Bentham*, 11 vols. (Edinburgh: William Tait, 1838–1843).

Brecher, Bob. *Torture and the Ticking Bomb* (Oxford: Blackwell, 2007).

Brougham, Henry. *Speeches of Henry, Lord Brougham*, Volume 2 (Edinburgh: Adam and Charles Black, 1838).

Capaldi, Nichola. *John Stuart Mill* (Cambridge: Cambridge University Press, 2004).

Carwardine, William. *The Pullman Strike* (Chicago: Charles H. Kerr, 1971 [1894]).

Cleveland, Grover. *Presidential Problems* (London: G. P. Putnam's Sons, 1904).

Conradi, Peter. *Murdoch: A Life* (London: HarperCollins, 2001).

Conway, Stephen. "Bentham on Peace and War." *Utilitas* 1, no. 1 (1989): 82–201.

Crisp, Roger. *Mill on Utilitarianism* (London: Routledge, 1997).

Crisp, Roger A. "Third Method of Ethics?" *Philosophy and Phenomenological Research* (2012).

Crowdy, Terry. *Deceiving Hitler* (Oxford: Osprey, 2008).

Cushman, F., and E. Schwitzgebel. "Expertise in Moral Reasoning?" *Mind & Language* 27 (2012): 135–53.

Cushman, F., I. Young, and M. Hauser. "The Role of Reasoning and Intuition in Moral Judgments." *Psychological Science* 17 (12): 1082–89.

Damasio, Antonio. *Descartes' Error* (London: Picador, 1995).

Dancy, Jonathan. *Moral Reasons* (Oxford: Blackwell, 1993).

Dancy, Jonathan. *Ethics Without Principles* (Oxford: Clarendon Press, 2004).

Danziger, S., J. Levav, and K. Avnaim-Pesso. "Extraneous Factors in Judicial Decisions." Proceedings of the National Academy of Sciences, April 2011.

Darley, J. M., and C. D. Batson. "'From Jerusalem to Jericho': A Study of situational and dispositional variables in helping behavior." *Journal of Personality and Social Psychology* 27 (1973): 100–108.

De Dreu, Carsten, et al. "Oxytocin Promotes Human Ethnocentrism." *Proceedings of the National Academy of Sciences* 108, no. 4 (January 25, 2011): 1262–66.

Dershowitz, A. *Why Terrorism Works* (New Haven, CT: Yale University Press, 2002).

Dinwiddy, J. R. "Bentham and the Early Nineteenth Century." *The Bentham Newsletter* viii (1984).

Dooley, Gillian, ed. *From a Tiny Corner in the House of Fiction* (Columbia: South Carolina Press, 2003).

Dostoyevsky, F. *The Brothers Karamazov*. Translated by R. Pevear and L. Volokhonsky (New York: Vintage Classics, 1991).

Eagleman, D. "The Brain on Trial." *Atlantic Magazine*, Atlantic Monthly Group, July/August 2011. Available online at http://www.theatlantic.com/magazine/archive/2011/07/the-brain-on-trial/308520/

Edmonds, D., and J. Eidinow. *Wittgenstein's Poker* (London: Faber, 2001).

Edmonds, D., and N. Warburton, eds. *Philosophy Bites* (Oxford: Oxford University Press, 2010).

Feser, Edward. *Aquinas* (Oxford: One World, 2009).

Foot, M.R.D. *Memories of an SOE Historian* (Barnsley: Pen & Sword Military, 2008).

Foot, Philippa. "The Problem of Abortion." *Oxford Review* 5 (1967).

Foot, Philippa. *Natural Goodness* (Oxford: Clarendon, 2001).

Foot, Philippa. *Moral Dilemmas* (Oxford: Clarendon, 2002).

Foot, Philippa. *Virtues and Vices* (Oxford: Clarendon, 2002).

Fuller, Catherine, ed. *The Old Radical: Representations of Jeremy Bentham* (London: University College, 1998).

Glover, Jonathan. *Humanity: A Moral History of the Twentieth Century* (London: Pimlico, 2001).

Greene, J., S. Morelli, K. Lowenberg, L. Nystrom, and J. Cohen. "Cognitive Load Selectively Interferes with Utilitarian Moral Judgment." *Cognition* 107 (2008): 1144–54.

Greene, J., L. Nystrom, A. Engell, J. Darley, and J. Cohen. "The Neural Bases of Cognitive Conflict and Control in Moral Judgment." *Neuron* 44 (2004): 389–400.

Greene, J., B. Sommerville, L. Nystrom, J. Darley, and J. Cohen. "An fMRI Investigation of Emotional Engagement in Moral Judgment. *Science* 293 (2001): 2105–8.

Haidt, J. "The Emotional Dog and Its Rational Tail." *Psychological Review* 108, no. 4 (October 2001): 814–34.

Hanson, Neil. *The Custom of the Sea* (London: Corgi, 2000).

Hare, Richard. *The Language of Morals* (Oxford: Oxford University Press. 1975 [1952]).

Hare, Richard. *Moral Thinking* (Oxford: Clarendon Press, 1981).

Harrison, Ross. *Bentham* (London: Routledge & Kegan Paul, 1983).

Hauser, M. *Moral Minds* (New York: Harper Collins, 2006).

Hauser, M., F. Cushman, L. Young, R. Kang-Xing Jin, and J. Mikhail. "A Dissociation Between Moral Judgments and Justifications." *Mind & Language* 22 (2007): 1–21.

Honderich, T., ed. *Morality and Objectivity* (London: Routledge & Kegan Paul, 1985).

Hooker, Brad. *Ideal Code, Real World* (Oxford: Clarendon Press, 2002).

Hume, David. *A Treatise of Human Nature* (L. Selby Bigge edition) (London: Oxford University Press, 1975).

Hursthouse, R., G. Lawrence, and W. Quinn. *Virtues and Reasons* (Oxford: Clarendon Press, 1995).

Huxley, Aldous. *Brave New World* (London: Chatto & Windus, 1970 [1932]).

Jackson, A. *Correspondence of Andrew Jackson*, Vol. 4. Edited by John Spencer Bassett (Washington 1929), 146.

Jones, R.V. *Most Secret War* (London: Hamilton, 1978).

Kagan, Shelley. *The Additive Fallacy* (Chicago: Ethics, 1988).

Kahneman, Daniel. *Thinking, Fast and Slow* (London: Penguin, 2012).

Kamm, F. *Intricate Ethics* (Oxford: Oxford University Press, 2007).

Kamm, F. *Ethics for Enemies* (Oxford: Oxford University Press, 2011).

Kant, I. *Groundwork for the Metaphysics of Morals*. Edited by Lara Denis (Plymouth: Broadview Press, 2005).

Kass, L. "The Wisdom of Repugnance." *New Republic* 216, no. 22 (June 1997).

Kenny, A. *A Life in Oxford* (London: John Murray, 1997).

King, Peter. *Utilitarian Jurisprudence in America* (London: Garland, 1976).

Knobe, J., and S. Nichols, ed. *Experimental Philosophy* (Oxford: Oxford University Press, 2008).

Koenigs, Michael, et al. "Damage to the Prefrontal Cortex Increases Utilitarian Moral Judgements." *Nature* 446, no. 7138 (April 19, 2007): 908–11.

Lehmann, John. *A Nest of Tigers* (London: Macmillan, 1968).

Levy, Neil. "Neuroethics: A New Way of Doing Ethics." *AJOB Neuroscience* 2, no. 2 (2011): 3–9.

Liao, M., A. Wiegmann, J. Alexander, and G. Vong. "Putting the Trolley in Order." *Philosophical Psychology* 25, no. 5 (2011): 1–11.

Lindsey, Almont. *The Pullman Strike* (Chicago: University of Chicago Press, 1971 [1942]).

Lovibond, Sabina. *Iris Murdoch: Gender and Philosophy* (London: Routledge, 2011).

Lucas, P., and A. Sheeran. "Asperger's Syndrome and the Eccentricity and Genius of Jeremy Bentham." *Journal of Bentham Studies* 8 (2006): 1–20.

Magee, Bryan. *Men of Ideas* (London: BBC, 1978).

Matthews, Richard. *The Absolute Violation* (Montreal: McGill-Queen's University Press, 2008).

McMahan, Jeff. *The Ethics of Killing* (Oxford: Oxford University Press, 2002).

Midgely, Mary. *The Owl of Minerva* (London: Routledge, 2005).

Mikhail, John. *Elements of Moral Cognition* (Cambridge: Cambridge University Press, 2011).

Mill, John Stuart. *Mill on Bentham and Coleridge*. Edited by F. R. Leavis (Cambridge: Cambridge University Press, 1980 [1950]).

Mill, John Stuart. *Autobiography* (Halifax: Ryburn Publishing Ltd., 1992 [1873]).

Mill, John Stuart. *Utilitarianism and On Liberty* (Oxford: Blackwell, 2002).

Morris, June. *The Life and Times of Thomas Balogh* (Eastbourne: Sussex Academic Press, 2007).

Murdoch, Iris. *Under the Net* (Harmondsworth: Penguin, 1954).

Murdoch, Iris. *The Sovereignty of Good* (London: Routledge, 1991 [1970]).

Murdoch, Iris. *A Writer At War*. Edited by Peter Conradi (Clays, Suffolk: Short Books, 2010).

Nagel, Thomas. *The View From Nowhere* (Oxford: Oxford University Press, 1986).

Navarrete, C. D., M. McDonald, M. Mott, and B. Asher. "Virtual Morality: Emotion and Action in a Simulated 3-D Trolley Problem." *Emotion* 12, no. 2 (2012): 365–70.

Nietzsche, F. *Human. All Too Human* (Cambridge: Cambridge University Press, 1986).

Norcross, Alastair. "Off Her Trolley? Frances Kamm and the Metaphysics of Morality." *Utilitas* 20, no. 1 (2008): 65–80.

Nozick, Robert. *Anarchy, State and Utopia* (New York: Basic Books, 1974).

Otsuka, Mike. "Double Effect, Triple Effect and the Trolley Problem." *Utilitas* 20, no. 01 (2008): 92–110.

Papke, David. *The Pullman Case* (Lawrence: University Press of Kansas, 1999).

Parfit, Derek. *Reasons and Persons* (Oxford: Clarendon, 1984).

Petrinovich, L., and P. O'Neill. "Influence of Wording and Framing Effects on Moral Intuitions." *Ethology and Sociobiology* 17 (1996): 145–71.

Piaget, J. *The Moral Judgement of the Child* (Harmondsworth: Penguin, 1977 [1932]).

Pinker, Steven. *The Language Instinct* (London: Penguin, 1994).

Powers, Charles. *Vilfredo Pareto* (London: Sage, 1987).

Quinn, Warren. "Actions, Intentions, and Consequence." In A. Norcross and B. Steinbock, eds., *Killing and Letting Die*, 2nd ed. (New York: Fordham University Press, 1994).

Rachels, James. "Active and Passive Euthanasia." *New England Journal of Medicine* 292, no. 9 (January 1975): 78–80.

Reeves, Richard. *John Stuart Mill: Victorian Firebrand* (London: Atlantic Books, 2007).

Richter, Duncan. *Anscombe's Moral Philosophy* (Plymouth: Rowman & Littlefield, 2011).

Roe, Jeremy. *Gaudi* (New York: Parkstone Press, 2010).

Rorty, A., ed. *Essays on Aristotle's Ethics* (Berkeley: University of California Press, 1980).

Russell, Bertrand. *My Philosophical Development* (London: George Allen and Unwin, 1959).

Russell, Bertrand. *Sceptical Essays* (London: Unwin, 1977 [1935]).

Scanlon, Thomas. *Moral Dimensions* (Cambridge, MA: Harvard University Press, 2008).

Schultz, B., and G. Varouxakis, eds. *Utilitarianism and Empire* (Lanham: Lexington Books, 2005).

Searle, John. "Minds, Brains and Programs." *Behavioral and Brains Sciences* 3 (1980): 417–57.

Searle, John. *Minds, Brains and Science* (London: BBC, 1984).

Shepherd, J. "Mate Selection among Second Generation Kibbutz Adolescents." *Archives of Sexual Behavior* 1 (1971): 293–307.

Sidgwick, Henry. *Methods of Ethics*, 7th ed. (London: Macmillan, 1907; reissued 1962).

Simpson, Brian. *Cannibalism and the Common Law* (London: Hambledon Press, 1994).

Simpson, J. *Touching the Void* (London: Cape, 1988).

Singer, P. "Ethics and Intuitions." *Journal of Ethics* 9 (2005): 331–52.

Singer, P. *The Life You Can Save* (Oxford: Picador, 2009).

Small, D., and G. Loewenstein. "Helping a Victim or Helping the Victim: Altruism and Identifiability." *Journal of Risk and Uncertainty* 26 (2003): 5–16.

Smart, J., and B. Williams. *Utilitarianism For and Against* (Cambridge: Cambridge University Press, 1973).

Smith, A. *The Wealth of Nations*. Edited by R. Campbell and A. Skinner (Oxford: Clarendon, 1976 [1776]).

Smith, A. *The Theory of Moral Sentiments*. Edited by Knud Haakonssen (Cambridge: Cambridge University Press, 2002 [1759]).

Steinbock, B., and A. Norcross, eds. *Killing and Letting Die* (New York: Fordham University Press, 1994).

Suter, R., and G. Hertwig. "Time and Moral Judgement." *Cognition* 119 (2011): 454–58.

Tallis, R. *Aping Mankind* (Durham, NC: Acumen, 2011).

Teichmann, Roger. *The Philosophy of Elizabeth Anscombe* (Oxford: Oxford University Press, 2008).

Terbeck, S., G. Kahane, et al. "Propranolol Reduces Implicit Negative Racial Bias." *Psychopharmacology* 222 (2012): 419–24.

Terbeck S., G. Kahane, et al. "Beta-adrenergic Blockade Reduces Utilitarian Judgment." *Biological Psychology* (under review).

Thomson, J. J. *Rights, Restitution, and Risk* (Cambridge, MA: Harvard University Press, 1986).

Thomson, J. J. *The Realm of Rights* (Cambridge, MA: Harvard University Press, 1990).

Uhlmann, E., et al. "The motivated use of moral principles." *Judgement and Decision Making* 4, no. 6 (October 2009).

Unger, P. *Living High and Letting Die* (Oxford: Oxford University Press, 1996).

United States Strike Commission. *Chicago Strike 1894* (Washington, DC, 1895). Available online at http://archive.org/stream/reportonchicago 00wriggoog#page/n6/mode/2up.

Valdesolo, Piercarlo, and D. DeStano. "Manipulations of Emotional Context Shape Moral Judgment." *Psychological Science* 17 (June 2006): 476–77.

Voorhoeve, A. *Conversations on Ethics* (Oxford: Oxford University Press, 2009).

Wallach, W., and Colin Allen. *Moral Machines* (Oxford: Oxford University Press, 2009).

Warnock, Mary. *A Memoir* (London: Duckworth, 2000).

Waugh, Evelyn. *The Sword of Honour Trilogy* (London: Penguin, 1999).

Wedgwood, Ralph. "Defending Double Effect." *Ratio* 24, no. 4 (2011): 384–401.

Weinberg, J., S. Nichols, and S. Stich. 2001. "Normativity and Epistemic Intuitions." *Philosophical Topics* 29 (1 and 2): 429–59.

Wheatley, T., and J. Haidt. "Hypnotic Disgust Makes Moral Judgments More Severe." *Psychological Science* 16 (2005): 780–84.

Wiggins, D. *Ethics: Twelve Lectures on the Philosophy of Morality* (Cambridge, MA: Harvard University Press, 2006).

Williams, Bernard. *Moral Luck* (Cambridge: Cambridge University Press, 1981).

Williams, Bernard. *Ethics and the Limits of Philosophy* (London: Fontana, 1985).

Wittgenstein, Ludwig. *Philosophical Investigations.* Translated by G.E.M. Anscombe. (Oxford: Blackwell, 1953).

Wright, Nick, et al. "Human Responses to Unfairness with Primary Rewards and Their Biological Limits." *Scientific Reports* 2, Article number 593 (August 2012).

Ziegler Philip. *London at War* (London: Sinclair-Stevenson, 1995).

Index

psychology (*cont.*)
  Night Live test, 131; Ultimatum
    Game, 159–64; Zimbardo and, 128.
    See also neuroscience
psychopaths, 149–50, 164
Pullman, George, 57–60, 62, 178; and
    Pullman Strike, 59–60, 62, 158–59,
    178
purposefulness. *See* intention

racism, 128, 157–58
Ramachandran, Vilayanur, 147
rational choice theory, 104
Rationale of Judicial Evidence (Ben-
    tham), 72
Rawls, John, 95–97
"Reflective Equilibrium," 95–97
Refuge case, 170
responses: and gender, 92–93, 123;
    and political ideology, 92–93; and
    religion, 92–93; and socioeconomic
    class, 92–93; subconscious influ-
    ences on, 131–32, 141
responsibility: compatibilists and, 90–
    91; DDE and personal, 31
rights: Bentham on natural, 73;
    Greene and, 136; Kant and, 47–48;
    Thomson and, 39
robotic warfare, 123–24
Roozrokh, Hootan, 102–3
Ryle, Gilbert, 150–51

Scanlon, Thomas, 31
Searle, John: Chinese Room case, 171
self-defense. *See* self-preservation
self interest, 162–63
self-preservation: DDE and, 27–28;
    Zeebrugge Ferry killer, 119–21
self-sacrifice, 36–38, 51, 195n2
serotonin, 156, 158, 165
sex: brain tumor and sexual aberration,
    145–46; homosexuality, 61, 72, 109,
    148; mating behaviors of voles, 156–

57; as procreative act, 61; Roman
    Catholic doctrine and Anscombe's
    view on, 25, 61; sexual mores as cul-
    turally defined, 109, 148; sibling in-
    cest, 96, 133, 144
Sidgwick, Henry, 75, 78
Simpson, Brian, 119
Singer, Peter, 52, 82, 143, 148
Six Behind One case, 54–56, 55
Smith, Adam, 162–63
social psychology *See also* x-phi, 88–
    89, 128–39
Sophie's Choice (film), 121
Spur scenario, 8–10, 9; *vs.* Drug and
    Transplant cases, 33–34; *vs.* Fat
    Man, 38–43, 74, 82–83, 93, 106–7,
    177; *vs.* Loop, 42, 105–6; *vs.* Loop
    case, 63–64; *vs.* Six Behind One
    case, 54–55
Stanford Prison Experiment, 128
strikes (Pullman), 59–60, 62, 158–59,
    178
subconscious influences on responses,
    131–32, 141
subjectivism, 13–15, 34, 194n3
suicide, 195n2
surveys, 92–93

Tele-Transporter case, 170–71
terrorism, 49–50
A Theory of Justice (Rawls), 95–97
The Theory of Moral Sentiments
    (Smith), 162–63
The Republic (Plato), 169
Thomson, Judith Jarvis, 35–39, 42–43,
    176–77; "A Defense of Abortion,"
    39; dying violinist case, 39; falling
    ceiling case, 89; Loop case, 41, 42–
    43, 105; "The Trolley Problem,"
    35–38
thought experiments: limits of, 171;
    Locke's cobbler and prince, 170;
    moral intuition and, 171, 174; Nazi